PRESIDENT WILSON

BY

DANIEL HALÉVY

TRANSLATED FROM THE FRENCH
BY
HUGH STOKES

NEW YORK: JOHN LANE COMPANY
LONDON: JOHN LANE, THE BODLEY HEAD
MCMXIX

Press of
J. J. Little & Ives Company
New York, U. S. A.

PRESIDENT WILSON

PREFACE

At any other time the author would ask indulgence for presenting to the public such a summary work upon so difficult and vast a subject. But, with events crowding upon each other so rapidly that we can scarcely follow them, information can only be conveyed in a hasty and improvised manner.

The author has made use of two biographies: "Woodrow Wilson, the Man and His Work," by Mr. Henry Jones Ford, and "President Wilson, His Problems and His Policy," by Mr. H. Wilson Harris. He has had access to the fine library of the American Chamber of Commerce, always hospitable to workers. He has also been greatly helped by former colleagues of the Bureau des Études de la Maison de la Presse, MM. Othon Guerlac, Professor of French Literature at Cornell University, and M. Michel Beer. They have assisted him with advice, and opened for his benefit archives which are extremely valuable in the study of our own period.

D. H.

October, 1917.

CONTENTS

CHAPTER   PAGE

I.—CHILDHOOD AND YOUTH   9

II.—ESSAYIST AND HISTORIAN, 1890–
1902   36

III.—THE PRESIDENCY OF PRINCETON .   65

IV.—THE GOVERNMENT OF NEW JERSEY   84

V.—THE FIRST PRESIDENTIAL CANDIDA-
TURE   111

VI.—THE PRESIDENCY: REFORMS . . .   135

VII.—PRESIDENT WILSON AND WAR . .   154

VIII.—TOWARDS WAR: DEEDS   182

IX.—TOWARDS WAR: DOCTRINES . . .   215

X.—RE-ELECTION   231

XI.—WAR   254

THE most active of the aristocracies which take the lead in the United States of America is formed of the descendants of the puritan families. They have created manners, culture, the State itself. Woodrow Wilson belongs to these families by double kinship.

His grandfather, James Wilson, came originally from Ulster. In 1807, while quite a young man, he disembarked at Philadelphia. He was a man of the people, but well informed like so many members of the Protestant sects. Setting up as a printer, he was successful in business. In 1808 he married a girl, also an Ulster Presbyterian, who had crossed the Atlantic with him in the previous year. Then, leaving Philadelphia, they settled in Ohio where pioneers were busily founding the early townships. James Wilson established in Ohio a newspaper, the *Western Herald*. In 1832 he established a second, the *Pennsylvania Advocate* of Pittsburg. Both were produced with the assistance of his sons, who were brought up to be working printers as well as publicists.

This Anglo-Saxon humanity assumed its primitive aspect whilst conquering a world of virgin forests and marshy prairies, of mountains and of deserts.

> Be strong backed, brown handed, upright as your pines,
> By the shape of a hemisphere shape your designs.

Thus taught an old American verse that the child Wilson had often heard inculcated. These lines he learnt to repeat.

A man who works with his hands must explore, discover, clear the soil, cultivate, build, and guard his domain. The same type of man belonging to the intellectual classes preaches, teaches, publishes, edits, and prints. This was the case with the Wilsons, from father to son. James Wilson died a man of consideration and importance in his State. He had been nominated a magistrate, and was commonly called "Judge Wilson."

His youngest son, Joseph Ruggles Wilson, taught in the universities, becoming a pastor as well as a professor. His life was divided between these two occupations. He married Janet Woodrow, also of Presbyterian origin, her father being a Scottish pastor. In this household Thomas Woodrow Wilson was born on December 28, 1856. He grew up in a double atmosphere, American and European, in the somewhat rude freedom of the new world, in the already classical culture of the old.

These Puritan families were by no means of a grave and frowning temperament. Their blood, springing from Scotland and Ireland, was Celtic. It is a very brisk strain. England draws many of its public entertainers from Ireland. The Scotch are pre-eminent for the flow and beauty of their speech. Gladstone and Carlyle were of Scottish race. The Reverend Joseph Ruggles Wilson was famous for intellect and eloquence, and his son Woodrow Wilson has inherited both these gifts. They were perhaps increased, or, better still, developed by the manner of life in those southern states—Virginia, Tennessee, South Carolina—where the Rev. J. R. Wilson followed his pastoral and professorial career and educated his children. The culture was often very advanced, the literary taste often very refined, in these southern lands ruled by an old and rich rural aristocracy. Woodrow Wilson profited from these traditions and fortuitous combinations.

I cannot find in the stories of his biographers any characteristic which distinguishes his infancy and adolescence from those of children in general. He was a young Anglo-Saxon, well gifted, who was formed and strengthened in the traditions of his race. Like many others he had a passion for the sea, and wished to become a sailor. And he had a similar enthusiasm for bodily exercise, in which he excelled. He had little taste for science, but on the other hand a great inclination for reading, —historical, philosophical, and literary. Writing became his dominating interest, and this increased and did not change. At the age of twenty-one he became a member of the editorial committee which directed a magazine published by his fellow students at Princeton University. At twenty-two he was the sole editor, and carried off a prize for literature with an essay on Pitt. We would like to have young Wilson's judgment upon the great English leader, the dictator of the wars directed by England against revolutionary and Napoleonic imperialism. But it has not been possible to recover this essay.

Woodrow Wilson became a writer, and a political writer. This was his true vocation, in which he commenced his career. He was young, sagacious, and alert. He knew how to observe; and matter for observation was not lacking. From his earliest days he was surrounded by material which interested him and educated his mind. Woodrow Wilson was developing in the Southern States at the moment of the great crisis of his country in the nineteenth century. The Southern States owned slaves. The Northern States had none. The Southerners wished to keep their slaves, and to maintain—separate from their civic and family life—an inferior race. The Northerners desired to limit, even to suppress, an institution with such grave moral and social inconveniences. And the conflict had other ramifications. The Southerners defended at the same time, not simply a servile institution, but the right of each state forming part of the United States to govern itself in accordance with its own particular laws. They withdrew from the North and formed a separate Union. The men of the North, in fighting these seceding states, fought not only for the freedom of the blacks but also for the intangible character of the United States, the solidarity and the future of this state-union, which had been founded in order that millions of men might be assured a peaceful development across the full extent of an entire continent. The stakes in such a combat were immense, and the fight was carried on with extreme energy. The war of the Secession lasted four years,

from 1861 to 1865, and the early childhood
of Thomas Woodrow Wilson was shadowed
by the tragedy. Once, at the age of four, he
was playing by an open window and heard the
conversation of two men in the street outside.

"Have you heard the news?" said one.
"Lincoln has been elected President."

"Lincoln President?" replied the other.
"There'll be war."

These solemn words so impressed the child
that he never forgot them. There was indeed
war, and a terrible war. It exhausted men
and money. Had the Southerners been victorious North America would have become a new
Europe, divided into rival nations and con-
demned to the enfeebling fatigue of hatred
and of conflict. But they were conquered, and
the formal unity of America was saved.

Formal unity, let it be said. The real unity
was almost wholly to be created, or to be re-
created. The years following the War of Secession were equally difficult and sad. Amidst
these difficulties and this unhappiness Woodrow Wilson conceived his first political reflections. Thoughts were still in revolt, and institutions were hardly tested. What was the
value of these institutions? Europe had admired them, America was vain of them. Perhaps it had been wiser to admire the excellence

of the civic habits which distinguished the
English-speaking populations, the happiness of
a people for whom political shocks were very
diminished by reason of the resources and in-
finite immensity of the territory across which
they were scattered.   The Constitution of the
United States has some original and useful features.   For example, the Supreme Court which
has ended so many conflicts and the happy and
novel federal arrangements.   But this Constitution, on the other hand, is an ingenious
school exercise composed by some of Montesquieu's pupils.   Montesquieu had explained
the rare virtues of the English constitution in
its division of power, resulting in a liberating
strength.   Executive power is separate from
legislative power; the two Houses and the
King counter-balance, holding each other mutually in check, exercising one upon the other
an incessant control which blocks any attempt
at tyranny.   The American colonists wished
to forestall all tyranny, and Montesquieu was
their advisor.   They maintained the independence of the States, and, in the federal government, they introduced, and multiplied, independent wheels.   Judicial power had its
proper source and independence; in the same
manner the presidential power, and that of the
House of Representatives and also of the Sen-

ate. The House and the Senate voted the laws but had nothing to do with their execution. The President carried them out with the assistance of his chosen ministers. The ministers had nothing to do with the making of the laws. They received them ready made as a manager receives the orders of his master. The President could veto a law voted by the Congress. But if the two chambers upheld it with a majority of one-third the President was bound to accept and execute it. These conflicts have been by no means rare. The Constitution appears to have been made to provoke them, and to render them bitter. The American President does not spring from the chambers as does the French president. He is found amongst the people, and it very frequently happens that he does not belong to the party dominating the chambers. The whole machinery has been ingeniously built up for the destruction of power and the annihilation of government. It is the masterpiece of the political philosophy of the eighteenth century. During the War of Secession the two parties corrected the faults of their traditional politics by raising dictators. Lincoln, elected President by the North, was an admirable dictator with authority and prudence. But upon the return of peace, and with Lincoln assassinated, the old institutions regained their empire and displayed their weakness. The Southern States had to be reconciled, their return to freedom required regulation without too much delay. In the midst of an extreme disorder wisdom and coolness were very necessary. The two houses were of one opinion, the President of another. The chambers looked for increased vigour and further vengeance, the President desired continued indulgence and firmer union. Congress refused to listen to the cautious warnings which came from President Johnson, and the President opposed their laws with his veto. Congress, being master of the laws, insisted upon them. President Johnson, being master of the execution of the laws, busied himself in destroying them. He had his following in the country. He travelled from town to town, making speeches, and insulting the House of Representatives, a body he described as "hanging on the verge of government." The House accused him of High Treason. The Senate, being the judges of the case, acquitted him. Disorder followed, whilst the country awaited a promised reconstruction. In the South the massed negroes, under the direction of political adventurers, seemed to threaten the civilisation even of the old states of Virginia and

Georgia. In the North the demobilised soldiers attached to the victorious party cried for help and spoils after the war. Congress voted them extravagant pensions, offices were distributed as rewards, and demoralisation seized all the services of the State.

Such were the facts which furnished material for the reflections of the youthful Wilson in and about his twentieth year (1876). A book must be mentioned which added to the facts and quickened the reflections, namely, Bagehot's essay on *The English Constitution*. Bagehot was a banker who devoted his leisure to political authorship. He endeavoured to find the veritable springs of this famous and deeply studied Constitution. He attacked Montesquieu's ideas, showing them to possess neither foundation nor reality. He was strongly persuaded that the function of power is action, and that action is possible only if energy be concentrated. Montesquieu had shown how energy was dispersed in the English constitution, and had praised this aspect. In contradiction to Montesquieu, Bagehot had discovered and praised a concentration of energy. He did not ignore, nor did he detract from, the peculiarly English utility of the royal power. He was in no sense a jacobin. But he saw in the practical constitution of the English state a Chamber which had power, and in this Chamber a party which had a majority. And this party was able to nominate a prime minister, who selected his collaborators and governed with their aid. The result was what Bagehot called "cabinet government." "The Americans of 1787," he wrote, "thought they were copying the English Constitution, but they were contriving a contrast to it. Just as the American is the type of *composite* governments, in which the supreme power is divided between many bodies and functionaries, so the English is the type of *simple* constitutions, in which the ultimate power upon all questions is in the hands of the same persons."

The youthful Wilson read, observed, and thoroughly grasped the lesson taught by books and facts. His character was one of authority. Muddle was repugnant to him. His intelligence was of a decisive nature; he loved to reason matters out to a conclusion. At the age of twenty-three he published in the *International Review* for August, 1879, an article entitled "Cabinet Government in the United States." This essay, written under the influence of Bagehot, reveals a clear knowledge of one of the problems which were about to occupy the whole of his life.

"Our patriotism [he wrote] seems of late

to have been exchanging its wonted tone of confident hope for one of desponding solicitude. Anxiety about the future of our institutions seems to be daily becoming stronger in the minds of thoughtful Americans. A feeling of uneasiness is undoubtedly prevalent, sometimes taking the shape of a fear that grave, perhaps radical, defects in our mode of government are militating against our liberty and prosperity. A marked and alarming decline in statesmanship, a rule of levity and folly instead of wisdom and sober forethought in legislation, threaten to shake our trust not only in the men by whom our national policy is controlled, but also in the very principles upon which our Government rests. Both State and National legislatures are looked upon with nervous suspicion, and we hail an adjournment of Congress as a temporary immunity from danger."

In France we should call such language reactionary. But care must be taken not to employ too quickly words whose use is customary.

Wilson observed around him a disposition to "throw discredit upon the principle of which the practice has been considered the honour and political glory of America—the right of every man to a voice in the government under which he lives." But it was a disposition with-

out importance. European democracies are
hindered in their development by remem-
brances, by the example of strong institutions
which have preceded them and which still sur-
round them. Discontent and dissatisfaction
thus inspired are inevitably fed and excited by
these souvenirs and examples. Instead of contriving and acting, instead of looking towards
the future, their thoughts turn to a past they
are unable to forget. Remains still exist of
former institutions which still seem to be part
of the present. Tempted sometimes to return
to them, the success of such ventures is medi-
ocre where it does not result in failure. And
these experiments, which are indeed reactionary, exhaust all faculties of imagination, of
action, of hope itself. But this temptation
does not exist for the American peoples. In
their short history they have known but one
manner of being, and but a single political tradition—that of democracy. They must disappear, or contrive and advance in the practice even of democracy. A good number have
vanished. Others will save themselves perhaps by contrivance and invention.

The youthful Wilson did not speak ill of
democracy. This would have been lost time,
and he had better work to be employed upon.
He enjoyed a strong and hopeful confidence

which forms one of his characteristics, and
is also one of the irrational, instinctive, and
incoercible forces of his race. He saw clearly
and defined the defect of the American constitution. That defect is the dispersion of energies, the concerted paralysis of power.

"There is no one in Congress to speak for
the nation. Congress is a conglomeration of
inharmonious elements; a collection of men
representing each his neighbourhood, each his
local interest; an alarmingly large proportion
of its legislation is 'special'; all of it is at best
only a limping compromise between the con-
flicting interests of the innumerable localities
represented. There is no guiding or harmon-
ising power. Are the people in favour of a
particular policy—what means have they of
forcing it upon the sovereign legislature at
Washington? None but the most imperfect.
If they return representatives who favour it
(and this is the most they can do), these representatives, being under no directing power,
will find a mutual agreement impracticable
among so many, and will finally settle upon
some policy which satisfies nobody, removes
no difficulty, and makes little definite or valuable provision for the future."

Direction is lacking. As Mr. Wilson felt

and spoke at the age of twenty so he will always feel and speak. A policy must be initiated. He wished it then, and the wish will continue. At the beginning of his career he discovered his problem and his aim. But the choice of a remedy will vary. The Executive and the Legislative being separated, the problem is to establish between them a subordination. There are two alternatives. The first is to subordinate the Executive to the Legislative; the second, to subordinate the Legislative to the Executive. In later life Mr. Wilson will practise the first solution. In his younger days he did not see the problem in this light. He remained under the influence of his reading, and the liberal and parliamentary ideas of the nineteenth century. He praised the methods of "Cabinet Government" in the English manner, that is to say the government of the state by a minister springing from the chambers and responsible to them. "The Executive is in constant need of legislative co-operation; the legislative must be aided by an Executive who is in a position intelligently and vigorously to execute its acts. There must needs be, therefore, a binding link between them. . . . Such a link is the responsible cabinet."

In 1880 Mr. Wilson published some essays on English politicians (John Bright and Gladstone) in the magazine of the University of Virginia. At the end of 1880 he left this University. He had knocked himself up through an excessive strain of intellectual work, and for a year he rested with his family. But he was without means and had to settle to a profession. He decided to enter the law, and, in May, 1882, established himself in the new city of Atlanta. Life ran very keenly and there was much business. His choice seemed judicious. Mr. Wilson installed himself quite modestly; his simple office is still to be seen. He did not succeed. Without doubt he had too much taste for public affairs to interest himself deeply in private business. He waited for clients, but he did not know how to seek or attract them. He could not set aside his old habits of observation, of meditation upon historical and political problems. He had made a mistake in selecting his career, which he recognised after a year's waiting. Quitting Atlanta he returned to a university to finish studies and become a professor. He worked for three years. In 1885 he was given the charge of a historical course at Bryn Mawr College. He was then in his thirtieth year. His apprenticeship had been long and varied, but not unfruitful. He proved it by publishing during the same year 1885 a book entitled "Congressional Government; a Study of American Politics." A French translation of this work appeared in 1900.

This book deserves our attention. Mr. Wilson takes up the thread again—and it is a sign of tenacious thought—of the observations and the theses he published in 1879 in his first study. Ten years of experience fortified and enriched his ideas. "Congressional Government" is not a youthful work. Reading it gives us the measure of the man, reveals the instinctive lines of his thought and their outcome.

The revelation is perhaps surprising. Little was known of Mr. Wilson before his Presidency, very little before the war suddenly conferred upon him the grandiose and unforeseen position of world arbiter. At first he was judged by those messages addressed to the American nation, eloquent pages glowing with religious and Christian thought and democratic idealism. But the note struck in these messages is quite different from the tone of Woodrow Wilson's political studies, what may be called his lay work. In his personality, as in his family descent, there seems to be a double tradition, a double inspiration, one religious, the other practical. On one side there is the man of action, the clear-headed politician who speaks in shrewd and concise language, who seeks truth alone and that only for the purposes of action. On the other hand we find a leader of the people, sacerdotal in character, who, addressing himself to the masses—to touch them more deeply perhaps, and the better to lead them (again and always for action) —speaks a solemn language and seeks the pathos of the old faiths. But the most active of the two personalities, the most constant, never sleeping, is the first. If the President's messages are read with care a political prudence can be detected, an authoritative and real ardour. But in the political writings we find nothing but politics. We use the word in its noblest meaning. A politician is he who has the vocation, the passion, and eventually the genius of country and of state.

"Congressional Government" is at first sight the intelligent and lively production of a disciple of Bagehot who, however, does not equal his master. The old London banker had an experience and a temperament very different from that of our young politician. But the personal note of the book, its superiority, invites comparison. Bagehot is an observer animated by curiosity, but Woodrow Wilson observes with a more passionate interest. He does not analyse every detail of the political machinery of his country for the pleasure of analysis and the discovery of unforeseen combinations. His object is modification and amelioration. Perhaps already he is being stirred by a remote ambition for action, in order to make himself master of the machine.

How do these powers—so wisely arranged —work in practice? A semi-religious respect had for a long while preserved the work of the founders of the nation from criticism. He broke away from this deferential tradition, and followed his own line of analysis with a radical lack of respect. Woodrow Wilson wished to demonstrate that the idea of the American Constitution is false, and that its results are absurd. The Constitutionalists of 1787 tried to separate the three powers, executive, judicial, and legislative. By opposing these powers their desire was to make them counterbalance each other in so perfect a way that they could never menace the liberty of the citizens. Their idea of the state was negative. They did not realise that the function of the state is positive and directing. Deprived of power and unity, a state cannot fulfil such functions. What happened? The Constitution has never worked. It has always been expounded and circumvented by politicians. One of the three powers is always straining itself to assure the mastery at the expense of the other two. In the year 1885 when Mr. Wilson was writing "Congressional Government," the parliament triumphed. The President was no more than head clerk. He no longer dared make use of the right of speaking directly to Congress; he no longer directed the legislative work of the chamber by his recommendations or vetoes. The two chambers succeeded in restraining and stifling his powers. The Supreme Court, which judged as to the very legality of the laws, was effaced, and allowed the legislative power to exercise the privilege of determining the nature, extent, and grounds of its own powers. Nothing remained. The House of Representatives and the Senate, which together form Congress, became victors. But it was a sad victory. Congress was able to reduce its rivals, but it was not able to overcome the laws enshrined in the Constitution. It was able to suppress the liberties of the Executive, but the Executive existed outside it, and was able to glide into office by a tortuous path. Congress was able to diminish and weaken the authority of the Secretaries of State. They continued to exist, however. The President appointed

them, and Congress was not able to eject them.
Congress was not able to hold those great debates of criticism and judgment which are the
glory, the prestige, and the strength of the European Parliaments. The House of Representatives had to resign itself to obscure and
confused work, divided into forty-seven committees (which form its traditional organisation) under the direction of forty-seven chairmen, each one the master in his limited domain,
happy to preserve his authority by oblique
methods of domination. Thus the primitive
constitution was overthrown. A curious disintegration reigned even in the institution
which prevailed over the others. The effect of
this disintegration was a continual adjustment,
pettifoggery, explanation, which has been an
unfavourable influence upon the American political character. "We have always had plenty
of excellent lawyers [wrote Mr. Wilson in
"Congressional Government"] though we have
often had to do without even tolerable administrators, and seem destined to endure the in-
convenience of hereafter doing without any
constructive statesmen at all."

"Constructive!" The word is frequently
used in the political phraseology of the United
States of America. They speak of a constructive politician, of a constructive mind. Such

politicians and such intellects are rare. The
need of them is often experienced and expressed. Woodrow Wilson was one of the
first to feel the need, one of the ablest to express it. Would America always be able to
continue without leaders and constructors?
The answer was an assured "no." She wanted
them in the past, and discovered it during the
difficult period of her formation as a state.
"Washington and his Cabinet commanded the
ear of Congress, and gave shape to its deliberations; Adams, though often crossed and
thwarted, gave character to the government;
and Jefferson, as President no less than as Secretary of State, was the real leader of his
party. . . . What with quarrelling and fighting with England, buying Louisiana and Flor-
ida, building dykes to keep out the flood of the
French Revolution, and extricating the country from ceaseless broils with the South American Republics, the government was, as has
been pointed out, constantly busy, during the
first quarter century of its existence, with the
adjustment of foreign relations; and with foreign relations, of course, the Presidents had
everything to do, since theirs was the office of
negotiation." From 1830 difficulties lessened.
The American people settled in comfort across
its vast domain. The political parties organ-

ised themselves, and succeeded in diminishing the presidential authority. When the presidential candidate came to be chosen, it was recognised as imperatively necessary that he should have as short a political record as possible, and that he should wear a clean and irreproachable insignificance. "Gentlemen," said a distinguished American public man, "I would make an excellent President, but a very poor candidate." A decisive career which gives a man a well-understood place in public estimation constitutes a positive disability for the presidency; because candidacy must precede election, and the shoals of candidacy can be passed only by a light boat which carries little freight and can be turned readily about to suit the intricacies of the passage.

Thus were the Constitution and the political customs of the Republic of the United States of America as they appeared in 1885. Woodrow Wilson saw the urgency of reform. The country was growing in strength and becoming conscious of its growth. And, with the same movement, the souls of the people were fortified by national sentiment. "The war between the States [wrote Mr. Wilson] was the supreme and final struggle between those forces of disintegration which still remained in the blood of the body politic and those other forces of health, of union and amalgamation, which had been gradually building up that body in vigour and strength as the system passed from youth to maturity, and as its constitution hardened and ripened with advancing age." The victory of the North, the defeat of the separatists, ended these juvenile vacillations. The Republic of the United States of America was henceforth one of the first powers of the world. But the political State, motive force of this power, remained a weak machine. How was its infirmity to be cured? During the ten years that Mr. Wilson was studying and working, he does not seem to have concerned himself with any other question. How could this crumbling and disintegrating State be given the necessary strength and unity? How could it find the personal authority, in a word, the leadership, which—and Woodrow Wilson realised it from that moment—is the condition of energetic national action, or of any other action?

"If there be one principle clearer than another, [he wrote] it is this: that in any business, whether of government or of mere merchandising, *somebody must be trusted,* in order that when things go wrong it may be quite plain who should be punished. In order to drive trade at the speed and with the success you desire, you must confide without suspicion in your chief clerk, giving him the power to ruin you, because you thereby furnish him with a motive for serving you. His reputation, his own honour or disgrace, all his own commercial prospects, hang upon your success. And human nature is much the same in government as in the dry-goods trade. *Power and strict accountability for its use* are the essential constituents of good government. A sense of highest responsibility, a dignifying and elevating sense of being trusted, together with a consciousness of being in an official station so conspicuous that no faithful discharge of duty can go unacknowledged and unrewarded, and no breach of trust undiscovered and unpunished,—these are the influences, the only influences, which foster practical, energetic, and trustworthy statesmanship. The best rulers are always those to whom great power is intrusted in such a manner as to make them feel that they will surely be abundantly honoured and recompensed for a just and patriotic use of it, and to make them know that nothing can shield them from full retribution for every abuse of it."

Reform was necessary. Mr. Wilson, in ending his book, proposed a project of reform. We know it already, for it is the same idea he expressed in his essay of 1879, and that Bage-hot had taught him. "Since Congress has over-come the two concurrent powers," he said, "let us recognise the fact, and celebrate the victory by disembarrassing it of the iron bands of the Constitution. Let us give it, as in the English Parliament, the right of selecting the leader who will direct his Party and govern the coun-try." Mr. Wilson deceived himself, and he rec-ognised the fact later. The reform he pro-posed was valueless, for it was without true foundation. Mr. Wilson's wisdom was dis-turbed by the traditions of the European nine-teenth century, by the example of that Eng-lish parliamentarism which produced such ad-mirable leaders as Disraeli and Gladstone. Mr. Wilson did not value exactly, perhaps did not measure at all, the vitality of the presiden-tial institution as it exists in the United States, based upon a popular vote renewed every four years. He judged it by analogy with the Presidencies and the Constitutional Monar-chies of Europe. At the moment of his ob-servations it was far from active. He believed it to be expiring. But it only slept. Wash-ington and Lincoln had occupied the seat and glorified it in the past. Why should its future be without glory? The nation remained attached to this institution by habit and with hope. To alter it was far from wise.

We cannot be surprised at Mr. Wilson's error. No student could have foreseen, no theoretical observer could have foretold, the rapid enlargement, the unheard of development of the presidential function. This spontaneous change is one of the most singular surprises of history. The seed had been planted in rich soil.

MR. WILSON'S work is easy to follow because it is logical. At the age of twenty, the events of everyday life attracted his attention towards the problem of the American state. He studied the problem for ten years, and it became the subject of his first book. And now, though remote and detached from it, he enlarged the scope of the matter and studied it more profoundly. In a retreat honoured by time he occupied himself with the problem to its fullest extent. The subject he desired to make his own was the essentials of a State, as manifested in its consciousness and moral sense. What is the English state, the German state, the French state? What were the mediæval and classical states? What is a Parliament or a bureaucracy? In short, what is a state, and what are its functions? After three years of investigation Mr. Wilson published a book entitled, "The State: Elements of Historical and Practical Politics." This excellent manual had a great success in American universities, and was soon translated into French.

It is not the work of a scholar, for Mr. Wilson does not toil over the texts, and seeks his information at second hand. It is not the work of an inventive thinker. Mr. Wilson does not strive to construct a theory. He adopts the formula in vogue with the sociological school. The book is one of vigorous and comprehensive intelligence, which sets out solidly and concisely conclusions drawn from all useful facts. He does not give a dissertation upon the nature of a state, or its origin, or the limits of its rights. His point of view is entirely positive, "historical and practical," as the title warns us. He considers human societies as organisms with laws, functions, and directing members of which the first is the state. By means of the state "society adapts itself to its surroundings and realises a more active life." The state is a directing organisation. This is the reason of its existence, and the more surely it directs the more valuable it becomes. "The essential characteristic of all government, whatever its form, is authority. There must in every instance be, on the one hand, governors and, on the other, those who are governed. And the authority of governors, directly or indirectly, rests in all cases ultimately on force." Wilson did not believe in the decline of authority. The functions of the modern state did not

seem to him essentially different from those
of the states of antiquity. Was he then actually a conservative, and had the experience of
a new world meant nothing to him? This was
not the case, and one of his observations must
be quoted. Authority, he considered, should
be exercised, and must be exercised, in a different manner to-day. "Government does not
necessarily exist by open force [he wrote].
And indeed, it is very necessary that there
should be some other foundation. Military
despotisms are becoming rare and more precarious. The people are no longer disinte-
grated as in feudal society and the ancient mon-
archies; they form massed bodies, and their
powers of assent or opposition are very great.
The power of the majority is the innovation
of the modern world. And *the statesman's
art to-day is to awaken, to arouse, and to direct this new force.*"

These words must be italicized. It is impossible to read them without immediately be-
lieving that at some later time they will find
their application.

This book on "The State" is the only scientific work he has written. It made his reputation. In 1890 he was called to the Chair of
Jurisprudence in the University of Princeton,
where he had finished his studies. He ac-

cepted the offer at once, and entered a higher circle in which he developed and fulfilled his university career.

The University of Princeton has existed since the year 1746. It is one of the most ancient universities in America. Only Harvard, Yale, and William and Mary are older. Originally a religious foundation, the University of Princeton was established by the Calvinistic Presbyterian Church to which the Wilson family was attached. It remained affiliated to that church, and for a considerable time followed the tradition of selecting its presidents from amongst the Presbyterian dignitaries. This rule was not departed from until the end of the nineteenth century. The names of Princeton and of its University often recur in the history of the United States. Washington's soldiers were beaten under its walls, and traces of the combat are still shown. In 1783 an assembly of the new states held session in its halls, and it was at Princeton that Washington wrote and issued his Farewell to the Army. The University is in the State of New Jersey which borders upon the State of New York. Thus it is able to share the life of both North and East, and to participate in the culture of that part of America which is closest to Europe and still remains attached to the older continent. A great number of young men from the Southern States customarily enter their names on its books. Thus it is linked to another and different America, which has a life with interests and passions of its own, its own history, manners, and local pride. Princeton University is in the highest degree a national University, with all the peaceful majesty of those old universities of Oxford and Cambridge, its ancestors and exemplars. In addition it possesses the wealth of American institutions. Old pupils, the *alumni,* cherish and endow it with gifts. Occupying a domain which covers some five hundred acres, its halls, libraries, residences, and laboratories are scattered amidst the verdure. The lake is nearly three miles long. Carnegie gave the money which was necessary for the enlargement upon such a scale of the River Milletone which runs along the estate. Old, rich, and active, the University enjoys a prestige which benefits its teachers and its presidents. Its professors receive much consideration in American society, and its presidents are invested with a very high authority.

Public life was the true vocation of Mr. Wilson. His new position at the university afforded him facilities which he made use of

without delay.   He set about making himself
known other than as a man of science or a spe-
cialist.   He spoke well.   This talent was the
result of long application and a foreseeing will.
His friend and biographer, Mr. Henry Jones
Ford, says that he cultivated his faculty for
public speaking with a view to public service.
He wrote well.   His style was refined and exact, naturally animated and persuasive.   His
father acted as a judge and adviser.   All his
writings were read to the old man who exacted
an absolute clearness of expression.   He
would stop his son—

"What does that sentence mean?"

The son explained with all the clearness of
which he was capable.   Then the father would
reply:

"You must say it thus.   A target must be hit
in the bull's-eye.   You are not shooting at birds
with small shot which spread over the whole
country." *

"My father taught me," said Mr. Wilson,
"to think in definitions."

Mr. Wilson wished to make himself heard.
He desired to intervene in the discussion of
ideas, in those high polemics which occupy and
exercise the cultivated classes of every coun-

*See a conversation with the President, by Ida M. Tarbell,
in *Collier's* for October 28, 1916.

try. Was Mr. Wilson at that moment planning a political future? The statement cannot be affirmed with any certainty, although many indications allow us to suppose it. As a youth he had thought of such a career. As a man was he likely to be distracted and turned aside from such a path? Was he able to forget an ambition so fully justified by education and natural gifts? We cannot believe it. Mr. Wilson is tenacious in his designs as in his views. He renounces little easily. But the entry to a political career is difficult. Professional politicians guard the gates very carefully. Where novices are not welcomed it is necessary to wait until increased importance permits the newcomer to impose himself. Probably this was Mr. Wilson's plan. He was thirty-five years of age. Life was before him, and his chances were exceedingly good. For a while he neglected political discussion. As a university professor he made himself known, and he dealt with the more general problems of pedagogy and the intellectual life.

These problems are well known to us. The same questions are propounded in the same years in the same terms in the United States as in France. A single movement of ideas animates both the worlds of Europe and America. What is the value of science? How can its utility, and its limits, be defined? What is the value of traditional culture? How can we agree the exigencies of a general culture with the technical education of youth? These questions have occupied and even divided French opinion, and it is interesting to have Mr. Wilson's judgments. These verdicts always coincide with those arrived at in France and in Europe by the conservative bodies of opinion. We need not conclude that Mr. Wilson is a conservative according to the fashion of the old world, for it must be remembered that American traditions and lines of thought are different from ours. Without seeking to classify him according to definitions which will not meet his case, and in parties to which he does not belong, we must listen attentively, and endeavour to understand his reasoning.

We have already seen that Mr. Wilson's reflections in the political field followed at first a clear direction. He believed that force, authority, and the independence of the State were social necessities to be fully guaranteed. In the teaching world Mr. Wilson selected his points of view, and insisted upon his ideas with the same quickness and lucidity. His first interest in the education of an individual was the social rather than the individual value which is likely to accrue. In 1893 he delivered an address at the International Congress of Education at Chicago, and he explained himself in clear terms. "There is a two-fold aspect of the educational question," he said. "It may be discussed from the point of view of the individual who is seeking professional instruction as a means of gaining a livelihood, or from the point of view of society itself, which must wish to be well served by its professional classes. The community will doubtless be inclined to demand more education than the individual will be willing to tarry for before entering on the practice of his profession." Confronted with these two points of view, "the self-interest of the individual, or the self-interest of the community," Mr. Wilson at once made up his mind. He did not think (as an Anglo-Saxon of the nineteenth century would naturally have thought) that the individual is the best judge of the education he personally considers necessary, and that the convenience of society is after all the sum of individual conveniences. On the contrary the needs of society are different and more important. "The practical side of this question is certainly a very serious one in this country [he wrote]. That there should be an almost absolute freedom of occupation is a belief very intimately and tenaciously connected with the democratic theory of govern-

ment, and our legislators are very slow to lay
many restrictions upon it. Our colleges and
universities, and our law and medical and theological schools have seldom endowment
enough to render them independent of popular
demands and standards." He asked that the
high schools and universities should acquire
this liberty, and succeed in insisting upon the
level culture which is necessary for organised
humanity. The task was incumbent upon
them, for the American state did not concern
itself about education. What should a university teach if it wished to be worthy of so
old and grand a name? Mr. Wilson examined
the problem in an article which he published in
the *Forum* for September, 1894.

"In order to be national, a university should
have, at the centre of all its training, courses
of instruction in that literature which contains
the ideals of its race and all the nice proofs and
subtle inspirations of the character, spirit, and
thought of the nation which it serves; and, besides that, instruction in the history and leading conceptions of those institutions which
have served the nation's energies in the preservation of order and the maintenance of just
standards of civil virtue and public purpose.
These should constitute the common training
of all its students, as the only means of school-

ing their spirits for their common life as citizens. For the rest, they might be free to choose what they would learn. . . . The world in which we live is troubled by many voices, seeking to proclaim righteousness and judgment to come; but they disturb without instructing us. . . . There is no corrective for it all like a wide acquaintance with the best books that men have written, joined with a knowledge of the institutions men have made trial of in the past; and for each nation there is its own record of mental experience and political experiment. Such a record always sobers those who read it. It also steadies the nerves. If all educated men knew it, it would be as if they had had a revelation. They could stand together and govern, with open eyes and the gift of tongues which other men could understand. Here is like wild talk and headlong passion for reform in the past,—here in the books,—with all the motives that underlay the perilous utterance now laid bare: these are not new terrors and excitements. Neither need the wisdom be new, nor the humanity, by which they shall be moderated and turned to righteous ends. There is old experience in these matters, or rather in these states of mind. It is no new thing to have economic problems and dream dreams of romantic and adventurous social reconstruction.   And so it is out of books that we can get our means and our self-possession for a sane and systematic criticism of life."

Such is the fundamental idea which he explains and develops in his pedagogic studies. This great American is opposed to what in Europe we are accustomed to call Americanism. He scorns the hasty work of the moderns, their superficiality and the self-sufficiency of their thought.   Pushing it aside, he seeks a remedy, and finds it in the constant advocacy of a knowledge of the past.

In October, 1896, at Princeton itself, commissioned to deliver an address at a university solemnity, he selected for his subject, "Princeton in the nation's service."

"I have no laboratory but the world of books and men in which I live; but I am much mistaken if the scientific spirit of the age is not doing us a disservice, working in us a certain great degeneracy.   Science has bred in us a spirit of experiment and a contempt for the past.   It has made us credulous of quick improvement, hopeful of discovering panaceas, confident of success in every new thing. . . . It has given us agnosticism in the realm of philosophy, scientific anarchism in the field of politics. . . .

"Let me say once more, this is not the fault of the scientist; he has done his work with an intelligence and success which cannot be too much admired. It is the work of the noxious, intoxicating gas which has somehow got into the lungs of the rest of us from out the crevices of his workshop—a gas, it would seem, which forms only in the outer air, and where men do not know the right use of their lungs. I should tremble to see social reform led by men who had breathed it; I should fear nothing better than utter destruction from a revolution conceived and led in the scientific spirit. Science has not changed the nature of society, has not made history a whit easier to understand, human nature a whit easier to reform. It has won for us a great liberty in the physical world, a liberty from superstitious fear and from disease, a freedom to use nature as a familiar servant; but it has not freed us from ourselves. It has not purged us of passion or disposed us to virtue. It has not made us less covetous or less ambitious or less self-indulgent. On the contrary, it may be suspected of having enhanced our passions, by making wealth so quick to come, so fickle to stay. It has wrought such instant, incredible improvement in all the physical setting of our life, that we have grown the more impatient of the unreformed condition of the part it has not touched or bettered, and we want to get at our spirits and reconstruct them in like radical fashion by like processes of experiment. We have broken with the past and have come into a new world.

"Can any one wonder, then, that I ask for the old drill, the old memory of times gone by, the old schooling in precedent and tradition, the old keeping of faith with the past, as a preparation for leadership in days of social change?"

This address created great interest, says his biographer, Mr. Ford, and was reproduced in many reviews and newspapers. The educative and moral value of science was then—as in Europe—a matter of study and debate. In these discussions Mr. Wilson's address was of outstanding importance, and his name was quoted as an authority. His fine oratorical gifts commenced to be known. Towns, colleges, associations of every kind sought for him and wished to hear him. Mr. Wilson lacked the movement, the warm passion, the inventive and lyrical imagination of a Bryan. He had not the familiar impetuosity of a Theodore Roosevelt. His word did not fascinate or captivate from the first moment of utterance. But, gradually improving, it at last forced itself upon and dominated its auditors.

Thus Mr. Wilson was sensible of a growing and well disposed public interest. He responded to this attention by writing some books of a public and almost popular nature.

In 1892 he had published an historical study entitled "Division and Reunion," which narrated, with the precision of a manual rather than the charm of a story, the history of the United States between 1829 and 1889. This book is excellent. Events are analysed and men's characters are drawn with a masterly touch. But it was a student's book and had no other aim. In 1897 he published his large biography of Washington.

His best literary work, it is in every respect excellent. The insight and success of the attempt prove the author's power. He wished to write a biography, almost a novel. He wished to tell the story of Washington, his family, his friends, his home, to make him live again—from birth to death—amidst a multitude of private and public events. He managed it without the reader experiencing the slightest sense of effort. The work has charm and strength, and that continuity which holds the reader to the last page. Mr. Wilson could have shown more plainly the limitations of his hero, whose nature was slightly narrow and dull. He saw them very clearly, and indicated them perhaps sufficiently. He was an image maker rather than a portrait painter. He desired to produce a book wholly popular and national after the fashion, in a previous generation, of Thiers and Guizot. This was the task he attempted, and he fulfilled it with entire success.

Here is the Virginia in which Washington was born. The colony was formed by English royalist families who refused to bow down to the Puritan revolution, the regicides, and the Commonwealth. Washington belonged to these families, which carried to America their old mode of life, their aristocratic and rural manners, their feeling for authority and feudalism. From the age of twenty Washington administered and increased the family estates. He explored and surveyed new lands beyond the forests and the mountains. He commanded the militia, and fought against the French troops and the Indians. When the London Parliament undertook to tax the American colonists, Washington, an English gentleman, felt that his rights had been injured. The militia armed, and elected him their leader. Washington had too much honour to evade the tasks proposed. He accepted, and became the general of the new States of America. He was given undisciplined volunteers. For five years he lived with them, creating soldiers and an army. He was often beaten, was never discouraged. He could not imagine abandoning the task he had undertaken. He held himself ever ready in the case of a supreme reverse to cross the mountains with the fragments of his army, and to retire to the unexplored depths and the liberty of the vast refuges offered by the American continent. His constancy prevailed. England became weary, and the colonists were conquerors and free. Laying down their arms they returned to their workshops and their fields. Washington returned to his own lands. The task appeared to be finished. It was not. The liberated colonists had not been able to constitute themselves into a state. They separated and quarrelled. Would America, like Europe, become the sanguinary arena of divided races? Or, on the contrary, would it become a union of free and settled peoples? All the Americans who wished for the latter turned towards the leader who had commanded them as a whole and secured their freedom. Washington heard their appeal. He had never wished to become a conqueror in order to produce a new discord in the world. He desired the establishment of a strong and armed state. "We are either a united people, or we are not so," cried Washington. "If the former, let us in all matters of general concern act as a nation which has a national character to support; if we are not, let us no longer act a farce by pretending to it."

Some colonies were gravely troubled. Extreme democrats refused to pay taxes. Moderate democrats hesitated to force them, and wished to restore peace by negotiation and diplomatic influence. "You talk, my good sir," wrote Washington to one of these moderates (Henry Lee), "of employing influence to appease the present tumults in Massachusetts. I know not where that influence is to be found, or, if attainable, that it would be a proper remedy for the disorders. *Influence* is no *government*. Let us have one by which our lives, liberties, and properties will be secured, or let us know the worst at once."

Washington and his friends succeeded in voting a new Constitution. The United States of America were given a government, an army, a justiciary, a federal chief. Then came the question of selecting the first chief, the first President of the United States of America. The people, who had the right of election, knew but a single name, that of one man—Washington.

He governed for eight years, always with

prudence and authority, and as a stern
guardian of the laws. Parliament and people often resisted him. When revolutionary
France entered into the fight against England
a powerful party wished to ally itself with the
new republic. Washington did not approve of
the French ideas, and opposed the alliance. He
was insulted and lampooned, yet the injuries
and the caricatures did not diminish his profound popularity. Proposals were made to
elect him President for a third term. He did
not wish for further office, but desired to retire and end his life on his own estates. So
far as any man is able to fulfil his task Washington accomplished his. For a few years he
was allowed to enjoy the existence of a country
gentleman. It was a life he preferred to any
other, and only the hazards of history had
troubled it.

Such was a career, of which it has justly
been said that it modified the idea of human
greatness. No one has told the story with
more interest and more nobility than Mr. Wilson. He was delighted, it seems, to express
throughout his book all that the old world be-
queathed of any value to the young American
nation. Clearly Mr. Wilson was persuaded
of the importance and the excellence of this

legacy. He sympathised with this gentleman who had founded a nation and resisted all demagogic enthusiasms.* And clearly Mr. Wilson was attached to old England by thought as well as by blood. We must take care not to draw wrong inferences from this book or from university lectures presently to be quoted. Mr. Wilson is profoundly an American, a man renewed through contact with the soil, with a new atmosphere, and ever ready for innovation. He is the son of an Amer-

*Mr. Wilson has no enthusiasm for the French Revolution. He allows this to be seen in his story of the life of Washington, and he expressed himself still more clearly in a study on "Burke and the French Revolution" which appeared in the *Century Magazine* for September, 1901. I owe a knowledge of this study to the help and vast reading of M. René de Kérallain, who resumes it as follows: "It is a sincere eulogy of Burke, and a spirited defence of his attitude towards the French Revolution. They make a mistake, argued the Professor [as to the President of to-day I do not know] who reproach Burke for having lost his head and not understanding that a drastic revolution was necessary to purge France of her abuses. But Burke saw more than France. He saw in the Revolution 'a revolution of doctrine and theoretic dogma,' of rationalism to excess, and all which logically follows." Wilson pointed out the epidemic and contagious nature of these principles. "If the French revolutionary doctrines [he wrote] *had* taken root in England, what then? They did not . . ." Burke, resisting as he did, spoke the true mind of England. And this is the conclusion of the article: "After you have seen and done your duty, then philosophers may talk of it, and assess it as they will. Burke was right, and was himself, when he sought to keep the French infection out of England."

ican, the grandson of an immigrant, who, pushing out towards the West, founded his fortune by the combined effort of his brains and his hands. He knew in what manner his country was linked to the old world. He knew exactly where it changed, and commenced to be itself. Listen to what he said, in May, 1895, at the fiftieth anniversary of the Historical Society of the State of New Jersey:

"What, in fact, has been the course of American history? How is it to be distinguished from European history? What features has it of its own, which give it its distinctive plan and movement? We have suffered, it is to be feared, a very serious limitation of view until recent years by having all our history written in the East. It has smacked strongly of a local flavour. It has concerned itself too strongly with the origins and old world derivations of our story. Our historians have made their march from the sea with their heads over shoulder, their gaze always backward upon the landing places and homes of the first settlers. In spite of the steady immigration, with its persistent tide of foreign blood, they have chosen to speak often and to think always of our people as sprung after all from a common stock, bearing a family likeness in every branch, and following all the while old, familiar family ways. The view is the more misleading because it is so large a part of the truth without being all of it. The common British stock did first make the country, and has always set the pace. There were common institutions up and down the coast; and these had formed and hardened for a persistent growth before the great westward migration began, which was to reshape and modify every element of our life.

"But, the beginnings once safely made, change set in apace. . . . Until they had turned their backs once for all upon the sea; until they saw our western borders cleared of the French; until the mountain passes had grown familiar, and the lands beyond had become the central and constant theme of their hope, the goal and dream of their young men, they did not become an American people. . . . The 'West' is the great word of our history. The 'Westerner' has been the type and master of our American life."

Mr. Wilson finished his speech by drawing a vivacious portrait of Lincoln, the hero of the West, a son of pioneers, a wanderer amidst forests and over virgin waters, great by the youthfulness of his intellect and heart, great in his wisdom, subtlety, and energy. These gifts of nature carried him to the headship of the people. "In Lincoln [he said] you have the type of flower of our growth. It is as if Nature had made a typical American and then added with liberal hand the royal quality of genius, to show us what the type should be." *

Washington and Lincoln, the two outstanding figures of the United States, have both been studied by Mr. Wilson. Their glory was due through merit. But they deserved it by something more than their merit. By a tragic chance these men became at the same time not only heads of the state but also heads of the army. Under the direction of Washington the Americans entered into the war which freed them. Under the direction of Lincoln they entered into the civil war which saved the unity, the accord, the combination of the New World. Led by these two men they sacrificed themselves and gave their children by thou-

*There is a delightful page upon Lincoln in the conversation recorded by Ida M. Tarbell. "Lincoln [said the President enthusiastically] was the incarnation of what I call Americanism. He began his career as a prairie politician. He came from the rudest stock. But everything helped to form him, inform him, transform him. He learned as he went along. He arrived, knew nothing, and suddenly knew everything. When he came at first he knew nothing of the East. But from his first speech he conquered it, as he showed that he understood it thoroughly. Until the day he was made President he lacked every attribute of a President. He was a man of the people—with genius. He understood the West, the conservative East, even the South. As for the North, no man of the North has understood it so well. A marvellous person!"

sands. They conquered, and the names of their leaders reflect the immeasurable glory they had all acquired. Blood has always a singular authority. It founds, consecrates, and dominates history. To these two names a third will be added in the future. Washington, Lincoln, Wilson! The first two are to-day ideals. A century has passed, revealing them as a whole, and permitting us to judge them. The first traditionally incarnates the age and nobility of the race; the second, a youthful renaissance of the race upon new soil, the rough zest of a pioneer people. How will Mr. Wilson historically appear in the future? To the future must be left the liberty of its judgments. We must remain content to learn the origins and development of this strong-minded and wise American, so different from his predecessors, a man of an intellectual type who formed his character in the New World he aspired to direct.

High university problems, and the history of the past, did not distract Mr. Wilson from his young and living country. He had political ambitions which he did not forget. But in the year 1897, marked by the publication of his biography of Washington, some events took place which attracted his attention. They must now be mentioned.

Mr. Cleveland terminated his presidency. There have been few so interesting in the history of the United States. Mr. Cleveland belonged to the Democratic party, and, like Mr. Wilson, to the conservative section of that party. As a President he had governed. He was intrepid, and possessed common sense. He saw things clearly, and never hesitated. Exterior problems he met with considerable importance, and dared to determine them. He peremptorily stopped the imprudent action of an American consul in Hawaii. He entered with authority into an energetic action against England which wished to impose itself upon Venezuela. He addressed an ultimatum, had war credits voted, and compelled England to accept the judgment of arbitrators. He had no less resolution when faced by his party. He succeeded in removing some thousands of public appointments from electoral influences, and refused to follow a demagogic financial policy. This refusal broke his career, and ended his presidency. Cleveland was a great man who had not been given full scope by opportunity. But if he did not do great things, he knew how to give a great example, and how to break the bonds which shackled the presidential office.

The example was not lost to such an ardent observer as Mr. Wilson. This professor, already known in America for his useful books and his sure and firm speech, was in reality a man of action and of self-contained strength. Cleveland's deeds interested him profoundly. He suddenly discovered in them the solution of the chief problem of American politics. He had searched for it in books and foreign tradition. He thought he had found it in an imitation of British parliamentarism disciplined by a prime minister, leader of his party, and head of the government. But no fact confirmed this theoretical suggestion. With the most lively interest he observed the quite different attempt of a practical politician, a president of the republic who energetically endeavoured to render his presidency effective. In March, 1897, at the moment when Mr. Cleveland relinquished power, Mr. Wilson published in the *Atlantic Monthly* a eulogy of startling warmth. "It is plain [he wrote] that Mr. Cleveland has rendered the country great services, and that his singular independence and force of purpose have made the real character of the Government of the United States more evident than it ever was before. He has been the sort of President the makers of the Constitution had vaguely in mind: more man than partisan, with an independent will of his own; hardly a colleague of the Houses so much as an individual servant of the country; exercising his powers like a chief magistrate rather than like a party leader."

Mr. Wilson then wrote a popular history of the American people of which we are to have a French translation.

"I have written this book in order to teach myself the history of my country," he said to his publisher, in handing over the manuscript.

"When," replied the publisher, "will you yourself begin to make history?"

His strength was being recognised. When the need arose he would be called for.

Mr. Wilson told his story from the earliest days to the present time. He narrates the arrival of the first colonists, and passes to that historical day in April, 1889, when the last piece of virgin soil was opened up to the last of the pioneers, who, camped with horses and wagons, waited behind the line of sentinels. On April 9th, at noon, to the sound of the bugle, the barriers were taken away, and a rough crowd flung itself across the last open spaces. In the morning Oklahoma had been a desert. Now it had become a state in the powerful Union. Nothing remained to conquer in the interior of the New World. About the same period the United States, teeming with population, commenced to overflow and to ebb towards the old worlds. Mr. Wilson touched upon the opening history of this new phase, Hawaii annexed, Spain turned out of a still remaining possession, the Philippines occupied. Mr. Wilson enumerated these conquests, and enumerated them soberly. His story has no imperialistic tone, but it is deeply and strongly nationalistic. It reflects the tone of a statesman who knows history and does not shrink from new destinies.

"Of a sudden, as it seemed, and without premeditation, the United States had turned away from their long-time, deliberate absorption in their own domestic development, from the policy professed by every generation of their statesmen from the first, of separation from the embarrassing entanglements of foreign affairs; had given themselves a colonial empire, and taken their place of power in the field of international politics. No one who justly studied the course of their life could reasonably wonder at the thing that had happened. No doubt it had come about without premeditation. There had been no thought, when this war came, of sweeping the Spanish islands of far-away seas within the sovereignty of the

United States. But Spain's empire had proved a house of cards. When the American power touched it it fell to pieces. The government of Spain's colonies had everywhere failed and gone to hopeless decay. It would have been impossible, it would have been intolerable, to set it up again where it had collapsed. A quick instinct apprised American statesmen that they had come to a turning point in the progress of the nation. . . . It had turned from developing its own resources to make conquest of the markets of the world. . . . The spaces of their own continent were occupied and reduced to the uses of civilisation; they had no frontiers "to satisfy the feet of the young men"; these new frontiers in the Indies and in the far Pacific came to them as if out of the very necessity of the new career set before them. It was significant how uncritically the people accepted the unlooked for consequences of the war, with what naïve enthusiasm they hailed the conquests of their fleet and armies."

III—*The Presidency of Princeton*

IN 1902 Mr. Wilson was forty-five years of age. He was professor at Princeton University. He was neither a member of the House of Representatives nor a Senator. He had made no tentatives in this direction, had no ambition or aim in sight. Yet in ten years he was to be elected President of the Republic of the United States. How was such a thing possible? How did he manage it? A Frenchman, knowing only the methods of the French democracy, finds more here than he can easily explain or understand.

In France politics are actually a profession, requiring youthful apprenticeship and the whole devotion of a life. The politician advances from one step to another, and our presidents (save one, Marshal MacMahon, who was from every point of view an exception) have constantly been parliamentary old stagers. It is not the same with the American presidents. Parliamentary influence is exercised in their election, and with much force, but it does not determine or dominate it. The president is named by the people, and the popularity of the parliamentarians is not so great, nor is their prestige so high, that they are able to impose upon the masses their own choice. In the States the political parties are well organised and very strong. They select the candidates. And often, in order to increase their chances of success, they avoid picking out exhausted professional politicians, and, going outside the circle, seek men of repute and respect, new names which are likely to appeal to the voters. We are speaking here more particularly of the presidential candidates, but the same remarks apply to the governorships of the states. Each of the forty-eight states forming as a whole the United States is free within its own borders and able to elect its own Governor. State Governors and President of the Republic are both important and eminent offices embracing political functions which escape the personal influences of the politicians, and thus enable university professors, soldiers, and even leaders of industry to entertain high political hopes. If this position is not at once understood it is not possible to understand the course Mr. Wilson has taken in his career.

In 1902 the Presidency of Princeton University was vacant. The presidency of a university is an office to which we can offer no analogy. The New World astonishes us at

every fresh step. The American universities
are great free corporations uncontrolled by
uniform laws. They make their own laws,
and are self-governing. Their existence is like
that of a financial company or an industrial
trust. They have rich patrons who give them
money and are in some respects the owners of
the stock of the business. These patrons and
protectors form a council which nominates a
head. He is the president of the university.
According to American tradition he is allowed
great power, because many of the patrons, being men of business, know that one condition
of success is the liberty and responsibility of
the directing head. A President of University, educator of five or six thousand youths,
master of a royal domain, of schools, muse-
ums, and lands, exercises a kind of intellectual
magistrature which renders him comparable to
the bishops of an older Europe. We have already referred to the prestige enjoyed by the
professors of a university. The president
finds himself in a truly eminent position. He
has the right—almost the duty—to give an
opinion upon all the moral and intellectual
questions which occupy the country. "No persons in the country," wrote Bryce in his work
upon the United States, "hardly even the greatest railway magnates, are better known, and

certainly none are more respected, than the presidents of the leading universities, Harvard, Yale, Cornell, or Princeton. . . ."

What president were the administrators of Princeton going to elect? Until then the constant tradition had been to choose a reverend pastor of the Presbyterian Church. Amongst its faculties the University included a theological school. As it educated the clergy it seemed proper to continue as a whole under religious influence. However, the temptation was great to select this Professor Wilson, who had much authority over his pupils, and who had also acquired by diverse means a strong hold upon the public. Professor Wilson did not allure, but he attracted. He had few friends—it might even be said that he was not personally known. But he had some admirers. Though distant in manner he was not unsociable. His tall figure, which lacked neither dignity nor ease, appeared at various gatherings. He knew how to be amiable with women, had indeed a taste for amiability in that respect, for their conversation alone was sought by him. In everything he understood he gave constantly an impression of at least perfect capacity if not of high superiority. He was willing to accept the appointment. He obtained it, and became President of Princeton University.

Upon entering office he delivered an inaugural address, in which he defined the task of a university:

"The college is not for the majority who carry forward the common labour of the world, nor even for those who work at the skilled handicrafts which multiply the conveniences and the luxuries of the complex modern life. It is for the minority who plan, who conceive, who superintend, who mediate between group and group, and who must see the wide stage as a whole. Democratic nations must be served in this wise no less than those whose leaders are chosen by birth and privilege; and the college is no less democratic because it is for those who play a special part. . . .

"There are two ways of preparing a young man for his life work. One is to give him the skill and special knowledge which shall make a good tool, an excellent bread-winning tool, of him; and for thousands of young men that way must be followed. It is a good way. It is honourable. It is indispensable. But it is not for the college, and it can never be. The college should seek to make the men whom it receives something more than excellent servants of a trade or skilled practitioners of a profession. It should give them elasticity of faculty and breadth of vision, so that they shall have a surplus of mind to expend, not upon their profession only, for its liberalisation and enlargement, but also upon the broader interests which lie about them, in the spheres in which they are to be, not breadwinners merely, but citizens as well, and in their own hearts, where they are to grow to the stature of real nobility. It is this free capital of mind the world most stands in need of,—this free capital that awaits investment in undertakings, spiritual as well as material, which advance the race and help all men to a better life."

To discipline, to form, to enlarge the mind— such is the task of a university. And, in the opinion of Mr. Wilson, there is no better instrument for this task than the classical languages of antiquity.

"They are disciplinary only because of their definiteness and their established method; and they take their determinateness from their age and perfection. It is their age and completeness that render them so serviceable and so suitable for the first processes of education. By this means the boy is informed of the bodies of knowledge which are not experimental but settled, definite, fundamental. This is the stock upon which time out of mind all the thoughtful world has traded. These have been food of the mind for long generations. . . .*

"Drill in mathematics stands in the same category with familiar knowledge of the thought and speech of classical antiquity, because in them also we get the life-long accepted discipline of the race. . . . Here, too, as in the classics, is a definitive body of knowledge and of reason, a discipline which has been made test of through long generations, a method of thought which has in all ages steadied, perfected, enlarged, strengthened, and given precision to the powers of the mind. Mathematical drill is an introduction of the boy's mind to the most definitely settled rational experience of the world."

Such were his general ideas, and Mr. Wilson knew how to draw the moral. He opened his work, and commenced to exercise for the first time that extraordinary faculty for pro-

---

*Mr. Wilson never loses an occasion to assert his faith in the educative value of the classics. The *Outlook,* for June 13, 1917, gives an account of a conference held at Princeton on the place of the classics in a liberal education. Messrs. Taft, Roosevelt, and Wilson sent messages to the conference in favour of classical studies. "We must not reject," wrote the President, "the wisdom of which we are the heirs, and seek our fortunes with the slender baggage we have accumulated. We ought rather, as much as we are able, to insist upon an intimate knowledge of the classics."

ducing reforms which characterises all his activities.

Princeton University had serious need of being taken in hand. Discipline was vacillating, and study feeble. Mr. Wilson looked into everything. His first care was the examinations, which he made more severe. He got rid of the incapables. This was but the beginning. He then occupied himself with the courses of study, which were revised in a drastic manner. The modernists in the university had suppressed the obligatory subjects of classics and mathematics. They had introduced an optional system which gave the young men the liberty to follow agreeable and easy courses. Before they were twenty years old they were asked to make a most difficult choice. Mr. Wilson reformed this system. "No doubt we must make choice among them, and suffer the pupil himself to make choice," he said in his inaugural address. "But the choice that we make must be the chief choice, the choice the pupil makes the subordinate choice. We must supply the synthesis and must see to it that, whatever group of studies the student selects, it shall at least represent the round whole, and contain all the elements of modern knowledge." He outlined his views, and had them adopted. Neglecting the details, his system may be summarily stated that each student had to take at least five courses of study, two obligatory and three within his personal selection.

But the best programmes are of little avail if the methods of work are defective. Mr. Wilson reformed these methods. The young men sat at the lectures from two to three hours a day. They were then left to their own devices, to reading, to sport. They were not guided, and had contact with their teachers only during the short and not very effective lectures. Mr. Wilson proposed a new system, the creation of little groups of students in association with a tutor or assistant master who would direct the work by regular conversations, by common research after the manner of the German universities. "If we could get a body of such tutors at Princeton," he said, "we could transform the place from a place where there are youngsters doing tasks to a place where there are men doing thinking, men who are conversing about the things of thought, men who are eager and interested in the things of thought." Mr. Wilson undertook to form such a body, and succeeded. He recruited a hundred distinguished and advanced scholars and installed them in his University. He looked for them himself, and found them in the United States and in England. Two came from France, and two from Germany.

The best method of work is valueless if concentration is lacking and application absent. Mr. Wilson's project was a radical reform, which he introduced little by little. "If to seek to go to the root is to be a radical, a radical I am," he said one day with force. He soon proved it. The Princeton students lived dispersed in the lodgings and boarding houses of the neighbourhood. Men of the first and second years formed themselves into very exclusive and jealous circles. American society, with its slight equality, tends to assume this attitude. Men of the third and fourth years, or at least a proportion of them, a chosen prime, lived in magnificently fitted clubs. Mr. Wilson decided that students of the first and second years should re-enter the university buildings to live there in fellowship with their tutors according to the plan followed at Oxford and Cambridge. The change was considerable, and he succeeded in making it.

His reforming ambitions were not yet satisfied. He wished to go farther, always farther, and to insist upon the whole of the students—those of the third and fourth years as well as those of the first and second—returning to the university establishments. This entailed the diminution and suppression of these great clubs, so rich and proud, and strong in many friendships. Their existence troubled his authoritative spirit which sought for unity. Without a doubt it offended some old puritan inclination toward equality which existed in his character. From the day he took the presidency of Princeton in hand (asserts his biographer, Mr. H. Wilson Harris) he had premeditated the destruction of these clubs. "The colleges of this country must be reconstructed from top to bottom, and America is going to demand it."

Did he speak as a university professor or as a magistrate? It is a new voice, a magistral voice, and beneath the President of Princeton appears the future President of the United States. In 1906, when he spoke in this manner, Mr. Wilson was considering for the first time with real precision the career in front of him. In 1909 President Roosevelt's term of office expired, and his successor would be designated in 1908. Mr. Wilson asked himself if he could not be this successor, and prepared his candidature. It was an early experiment, for Mr. Wilson soon recognised that the Democratic party, to which he belonged, would again propose the popular orator Bryan. He waited.

But there awoke in him an agitating strain
which could be extinguished no longer, and
which was little in tune with his characteristic
university prudence and caution. This feeling
was one of vehemence and passion, which
seemed to come to him from a larger, freer existence. American public life was disturbed
at that moment. Animated by the petulance
of speeches against plutocracy, President
Roosevelt excited and set fire to the national
soul. This must be remembered in order to
understand Mr. Wilson's ardent initiatives
within his university.

Mr. Wilson prepared his reforms in silence.
This is a custom from which he has never departed. When he takes counsel it is in secret.
In June, 1907, he read to his administrative
board a scheme of total reconstruction of the
old university. New buildings were to be
erected to correspond to the needs of a new
organisation. All the students would live with
their tutors under the same roof. The authority of his office, together with that of his
personality, were such that the board adopted
the project at once. But soon it became public,
and opposition became manifest. There was a
cry of indignation. The older members, those
alumni, whose gifts had given life to the University, did not wish the clubs in which they

had once lived, and which now sheltered their sons, to be touched. Many approached the administrative body. Others announced their intention of withdrawing their financial aid. The board could not resist the clamour. In October they asked their President to withdraw his scheme. Mr. Wilson was obliged to consent. But he specifically stated that he retained his views, and that he would not cease to fight his opponents. "It was then that I met Wall Street for the first time," he is reported as saying in conversation. "And I saw for myself the manner in which Wall Street opposes everything that is attempted for the good of the country."

Leaving for an instant a fight by no means ended, we will turn to a book, produced in a most elegant typographical form, which Mr. Wilson published in 1908. He entitled it "The Free Life," and the contents are a farewell with last wishes that Mr. Wilson addressed to the young men who quitted Princeton after four years of study. This *adieu* is in the form of a sermon. Such is the tradition of the place, he observed, and its observance is easy to him. As a child he had often listened to his father's preaching. At once he announces his text: "And be not conformed to this world: but be ye transformed by the renewing of your mind, that ye may prove what is that good, and acceptable, and perfect will of God." (Romans xii:2.) A mystical text, impregnated with the spirit of St. Paul, which is the very spirit of Christian protestantism. "Be not conformed." . . . These churches, which in the face of the Anglican church have heard and remembered these words, retain them as their title of nobility. They maintain a spirit of separation, of Christian protestation, and recognise each other as sisters by their common characteristic—nonconformity. "Be not conformed. . . ." This is the advice Mr. Wilson gives to these young men. They must listen to themselves, remain faithful to themselves.

"It is not a thing remote, obscure, poetical, but a very real thing, that lives in the consciousness of every one of us. Every thoughtful man, every man not merely of vagrant mind, has been aware, not once, but many times, of some unconquerable spirit that he calls *himself,* which is struggling against being overborne by circumstances, against being forced into conformity with things his heart is not in, things which seem to deaden him and deprive him of his natural independence and integrity, so that his individuality is lost and merged into some common, indistinguishable mass, the nameless multitudes of a world that ceaselessly shifts and alters and is never twice the same. He feels instinctively that the only victory lies in nonconformity. He must adjust himself to these things that come and go and have no base or principle, but he must not be subdued by them or lose his own clear lines of chosen action."

"Be not conformed. . . . Be yourselves. . . ." We know the formula, and many others which spring from it. They are old, and, to their age and the abundance of deeds they suggest, they owe an extreme malleability. Ibsen has drawn from them anarchistic morals. Mr. Wilson makes use of them to teach a very different moral. This descendant of the puritans, living in the magnificent establishment over which he presides, amongst classical buildings, sheltering groves, soft resting places, amidst the silence and the luxury of an American university, cannot shut his eyes to the moral. "Be not conformed to the world, to the usages of the world . . ." he says to the young men on the point of departure. He speaks to them not as a mystic but as a scholar. The world he warns these youths to be careful of is New York and Wall Street; the worlds of politics, finance, industry, the saloons, the party, the club. It is the whole secular world. "Be ye

transformed by the renewing of your mind,"
he cries. The views of a great scholar, of a
great teacher, are worthy of attention. *Renew
your minds.* What Wilson meant was: do not
forget the four years you terminate to-day, and
that you have been living in familiarity with
thought and the eternal.

"For four years you have been given an opportunity to get the offing and perspective of
books, of the truths which are of no age, but
run unbroken and unaltered throughout the
changeful life of all ages. You know the long
measurements, the high laws by which the
world's progress has ever been gauged and assessed,—laws of sound thinking and pure motive which seem to lie apart in calm regions
which passion cannot disturb, into whose pure
air wander no mists or confusions or threats
of storm. Amidst every altered aspect of time
and circumstance the human heart has remained unchanged. No doubt there were sim-
pler ages, when the things which now perplex
us in hope and conduct seemed very plain. If
life confuses us now, no doubt it is because we
do not see it simply and see it whole. Look
back more often, and you shall find your vision
adjusted for the look ahead."

It is not the appeal of an apostle, but the advice of a wise platonist. The apostle never

said: "Look behind, consult the eternal experience." He did say: "Look towards God, follow the revelation of the absolute." But the Anglo-Saxon spirit is clever to adapt itself to all things, to give heed to them, and to utilise them to the best purpose. The Anglo-Saxon spirit is practical, and makes everything serve its purpose. "Reflections like these [wrote Mr. Wilson] seem to spring naturally to the thought out of the words of Scripture counsel I have read." And his discourse goes on, continuing serenely to combine a platonistic paraphrase with an evangelical text. Transform your minds, he says; transform them by knowledge. Knowledge gives eternal youth. Transform them by friendship. Friendship is a royal gift, and the nobility of the soul. Knowledge and Friendship are to be found in the university.

"The transformed university man, whose thought and will have been in fact renewed out of the sources of knowledge and of love, is one of the great dynamic forces of the world. We live in an age disturbed, confused, bewildered. . . . There are many voices of counsel, but few voices of wisdom; there is much excitement and feverish activity, but little concert of thoughtful purpose. We are distressed by our own ungoverned, undirected energies, and do many things but nothing long. It is our duty to find ourselves. It is our privilege to be calm and know that the truth has not changed, that old wisdom is more to be desired than any new nostrum, that we must neither run with the crowd nor deride it, but seek sober counsel for it and for ourselves."

We shall not hear this language long. The University will disappear before politics and the magistrature. On March 9, 1909, Mr. Wilson spoke at the annual banquet of the Civic League of St. Louis. "The older I become [he said] the less and less fit I am to speak at banquets for I become more and more serious. I consider some of my friends with a hopeless envy. They are so measured in tone, so cold. Their judgments are always so separate from the active movements which animate them. As for myself, the older I become, the more I become ardent. . . ." This was evident at Princeton where the old combat was still unextinguished.

It became public. The New York journals commented upon it, and polemics commenced to which Mr. Wilson did not seem to be a stranger. The conflict at last assumed the singular form of a kind of duel between an isolated leader, almost at variance with his administrative board, and some millionaire patrons. In 1909 a gift of 250,000 dollars was offered to the University upon the condition that the sum should be expended upon the construction of a graduate school. The question arose as to the plans of the proposed school. Mr. Wilson still adhered to his old scheme, which had been adjourned but not rejected. Certain of the terms specified by the donor he considered contrary to his own ideas, and he asked that the gift be refused. "When the country is looking to us as men who prefer ideas even to money," he asked, "are we going to withdraw and say, 'After all, we find we were mistaken: we prefer money to ideas'?" He came into collision with a very lively opposition, and triumphed. The gift was refused.

His victory did not last long. Hardly had he disembarrassed himself of this offer of a quarter of a million dollars than a new offer of 3,000,000 dollars was thrown at him. Immediately the rejected quarter of a million was brought into the charge, and the gift again tendered. There were too many millions! Mr. Wilson gave way beneath the burden, and prepared to quit this presidency where he was at last conquered. But the defeat was not a humiliation, and, unharmed, he carried his ideas elsewhere.

WITHOUT a doubt Mr. Wilson considered from this time the possibility of becoming President of the United States. Perhaps we may take as a kind of programme the interesting addresses he delivered in 1907, and published in May, 1908 (a few months before the presidential election of Mr. Taft), upon "Constitutional Government in the United States." These vigorous and concise lectures have a double interest. They give an excellent outline of the American political organisation, and also form a masterly exposition of the ideas of the man who was soon to direct this organisation with all the strength of his will.

These lectures present us with a sort of new edition, very virile and ripened, of the youthful "Congressional Government." In both books Mr. Wilson examines the House of Representatives, the Senate, the Courts of Justice, the Presidency, the Parties, what they are, and the manner in which they work. He concerns himself less with the written law and more with the actual practice. He interests himself greatly in what is, but still more so in what is preparing, and what is going to be. An ardent and reforming zeal incites his observations. A political constitution, he tells us, is not a machine put together once for all, the subject of a definition or a mathematical demonstration. A political constitution is a living thing, and its study must be approached not in a mathematical or Newtonian spirit, as did the old theorists of the eighteenth century, but in a vital and Darwinian spirit, with a constant care to disclose the parts which are hidden, those which strengthen, those which modify. "Constitutions," he said loftily, "are what politicians make them." But there exists in the constitution of the United States one part which ought to be strong. This is the Presidency. Cleveland commenced an evolution which Roosevelt continued. The Presidents of the nineteenth century selected their ministers from amongst the more eminent politicians. Cleveland at first, and then Roosevelt following, changed the practice. They considered that the ministers grouped round the President should form a body of personal advisers, and that the President was in a position to pick them from amongst those who possessed his personal confidence and whose advice he preferred. Cleveland at first, and then

Roosevelt, wished to bring into association men whose power of work had been proved not only in public but also in private life, as, for instance, bankers who had never sat upon the committee of any political party, lawyers who had stood aside from politics, administrators who had succeeded in the direction of public services. Their attitude was as if the President alone had a public function, the ministers being but privy councillors, the collaborators of his choice.

This was not the only modification which increased the presidential office. Everything seemed concurrently to further its aggrandisement. The increasing difficulty and complication of foreign affairs, in which the President possesses almost quasi-sovereign powers, gave him in the eyes of the world the figure of leadership. His messages to Congress, in the old days very rare and quite unheeded, now became through this prestige most important documents of great weight with public opinion. The President thus acquired a power of direction and initiative, which, added to the right of veto given to him by the Constitution, completely armed him. The foundation of his power is national assent, and it is limited only by this assent. "The President is at liberty [wrote Mr. Wilson] both in law and conscience, to be as big a man as he can. His capacity will set the limit; and if Congress be overborne by him, it will be no fault of the makers of the Constitution,—it will be from no lack of constitutional powers on its part, but only because the President has the nation behind him, and Congress has not. He has no means of compelling Congress except through public opinion."

One danger threatened the office, a danger menacing enough to become overwhelming and crushing upon those who held it. It seemed that the entire nation fixed its gaze upon their President and awaited his words. Upon every question, no matter what technicality was involved, military, economic, or legislative, the President's knowledge and judgment were called for. He must know every problem, and be able to satisfy every anxiety. "Men of ordinary physique and discretion [wrote Mr. Wilson] cannot be Presidents and live if the strain be not somehow relieved. We shall be obliged always to be picking our chief magistrates from among wise and prudent athletes —a small class."

However, he was ready. He did not speak or make proclamation. He did not needlessly advertise his vocation. But it existed and pressed him forward, and was not likely to disappear. He conducted himself like a "wise and prudent athlete," and planned his life sedately. His time as a University President had not been lost. He had acquired a useful celebrity as a radical Democrat. He entered actively into political conflicts, and the fight he had had with his administrative board had rendered him popular. What would be his next step? We are at the beginning of the summer of 1910. At Princeton the conservative coalition, the plutocratic *alumni,* had been victorious. Mr. Wilson had to seek occupation elsewhere. The presidential election was timed for 1912. Would Mr. Wilson stand as a candidate? Possibly. Mr. Taft, the then President, was a capable and honest official who lacked strength. He most certainly would not be re-elected. Undoubtedly Mr. Roosevelt would present himself. What chance had he of election? His interesting and oscillating personality occupied public opinion and lent animation to the scene, but did not carry conviction. Mr. Roosevelt was a brilliant political adventurer, and could be engaged in the fight without rashness. Mr. Bryan, the Democrat, already twice a candidate and twice defeated, seemed hardly destined for success. There were fine chances for a new man, and we do not doubt that Mr. Wilson took them into his calculation. Nevertheless there were two years to run. They had to be employed usefully and with some striking result. The Governorship of New Jersey was about to become vacant, the election taking place in November, 1910, the candidates being selected in September. Mr. Wilson decided to make the experiment and become known as a Governor. "Undoubtedly," wrote his friend and biographer, Mr. Henry Jones Ford, "the movement which carried him from the Presidency of Princeton to the Governorship of New Jersey had for its aim the Presidency of the nation."

What is a State Governor? The French reader needs some explanation of the nature of his duties. The Republic of the United States is actually an old and permanent union of states. When they federated in 1775 to fight England there were thirteen. To-day there are forty-eight, and each exists as a State. Each one has its own name; its constitution as formulated by the first colonists and reformed by the inhabitants at their pleasure; its civil and criminal code; its fiscal legislation, and its working powers. It has its first and second Houses, and a Governor elected for two, three, or four years. The functions of a Governor are much the same, although on a smaller scale, to those fulfilled in the eyes of the world by the President of the United States. The promotion from one office to the other is natural and reasonable. In these later years there appears to be a growing tradition which inclines the American electors to select their federal President from amongst their forty-eight Governors. Mr. Roosevelt was Governor before becoming President. The precedent was good. Mr. Wilson decided to attempt in the Governorship of New Jersey the last trial and the last proof of his strength.

The Government of New Jersey is very important. A neighbour to New York, which it adjoins, its activity is inextricably mixed with that of the Atlantic capital. New York is built at the mouth of a wide river, the Hudson. It occupies one shore on one side of the estuary. New Jersey occupies the other. In reality they form the same city, separated by the historical hazard of a frontier. But this chance made a lot of difference. The legal control of financial corporations was not the same in New York as in Jersey City, less rigid in one, sterner in the other. The financial corporations and trusts knew very well how to avail themselves of so accommodating a neighbour. They crossed the river, registered themselves in Jersey City, and were troubled no more. The democratic politicians, who were masters in New Jersey, acted in connivance with the trusts and benefited from the hospitality asked of them. The benefit was unfortunate and lowered the entire political morality of the State. It was generally recognised that this morality was deplorable, and that the House, the offices, and the committees of the State of New Jersey were what we call in France "cavernes."

Into these dens Mr. Wilson, a university man of upright but distant nature, was about to enter as master. How could it be possible? In many parts of the old world we have these "cavernes," these dens of brigands. But the occupants know well how to guard their gates. They refuse admittance to any one likely to disturb them. And if, by any chance, an unsympathetic being does slip in they eliminate him by a wise quarantine. Have their American friends of the same type less prudence? No one will believe it. The difference of the political machine explains the difference between the possibilities of American and Continental parliamentarism. In America the heads of the executive power, the Governors or the President, are elected by universal suffrage. The politicians are very united and very strong. Our political committees do not equal their redoubtable machines which are in sovereign control of offices and favours. But with both Governors or President there is a great protection every three or four years which we lack, and which helps to balance the occult powers. The people, directly consulted, selects its Governors and its Representatives. This public appeal is a sudden burst of light and air. . . . We will not exaggerate. The politicians, committees, and their chairmen, what are known as "the machines and their bosses," play cautiously. They know how to reduce the efficacy of the appeal for protection, to pass the air and the light through a fine sieve. However, the process gives them trouble, and the result is not certain. They do not love the recurrence of these "Great Days" when the people name their leaders. They elude the verdict by manœuvres. One consists of hiding themselves behind a candidate who is not a professional politician. They choose a man capable of pleasing and likely to succeed by the novelty of his name, by a prestige acquired elsewhere amidst surroundings not discredited, a university chair or a court of justice, a man in fact of the type of Mr. Wilson who can be tempted by the brilliancy of high office. The politicians, who adopt him and push his candidature, count upon the inexperience of this newcomer, and on their knowledge of the world, to reduce him to impotency on the morrow of his election. They then are able to govern as they governed before. The situation is false. People, politicians, and candidates try hard to extract advantage from it. "The trouble with our present political condition [wrote President Wilson in "The New Freedom"] is that we need some man who has not been associated with the governing classes and the governing influences of this country to stand up and speak for us; we need to hear a voice from the outside calling upon the American people to assert again their rights and prerogatives in the possession of their own government."

The political "bosses" of New Jersey had every reason to be confident. Their moral discredit was an old and established fact. They had been many times denounced and attacked by very active and valorous civic leagues. They had always so well known how to defend their power that their adversaries were discouraged and the honest men of the State reduced to inertia. Mr. Wilson's ardour and eloquence were recognised. These qualities they judged would make him a good advocate. They did not forget his intellectual past and his ineffectual effort to dominate the adminis-

trative board of Princeton University. This
misadventure foretold a Governor easy to manage. Voluntarily they adopted him. The
"boss" of the democratic party, a certain James
Smith who was very discredited, consented to
retire, and promised that he would renounce
the representation of the State of New Jersey
in the Senate of the United States. It was
arranged that the brilliant "outsider" from the
University, the stranger candidate, should be
given every freedom, and should receive every
promise necessary for his success.

In the meanwhile Mr. Wilson did not interrupt his dignified professorial existence. He
was playing golf on the links of Princeton
when a messenger announced that his candidature was decidedly acceptable to the Democrats of New Jersey who were at that moment
sitting in party convention. The convention,
which had acclaimed his name, wished to hear
him speak. The messengers with these tidings
carried off Mr. Wilson in their auto, covered
eleven miles in half an hour, and placed him on
the platform where he opened his public career.
He spoke clearly and with a skill which must
have given rise to thought amongst the political old stagers who had just heard his name.
He did not waste his time in empty thanks, but
made it publicly clear that he had been named

candidate of the democratic party without so-
licitation or engagement on his side, and that
consequently he would be wholly free, if elected
Governor, to serve the people and the State
with entire independence. And he set forth
his programme.

"Above all the issues there are three which
demand our particular attention; first, the
business-like and economical administration of
the business of the State; second, equalisation
of taxes; and third, control of corporations.
There are other important questions that confront us, as they confront all the other States
of the Union in this day of readjustment, like
the matter of corrupt practices in elections,
liability of employers and conservation. But
the three I have mentioned will dominate the
rest. It is imperative that we should not only
master them, but also act upon them, and act
very definitely.

"The question of the control of corporations
is a very difficult one, upon which no man can
speak with confidence. But some things are
plain. It is plain, so far as New Jersey is concerned, that we must have a public service commission with the amplest powers to oversee and
regulate the administration of public service
corporations throughout the State. . . . The
regulation of corporations is the duty of the

State much more directly than it is the duty of the Government of the United States. It is my strong hope that New Jersey may lead the way in reform by scrutinising very carefully the enterprises she consents to incorporate: their make-up, their objects, the basis and method of their capitalisation, their organisation with respect to liability to control by the State, their conformity to state and federal statutes. This can be done, and done effectually. I covet for New Jersey the honour of doing it."

This clear speech was the first of a vigorous and brilliant campaign. Until November 8th, day of the election, Mr. Wilson travelled through the State, always setting forth his independence and his plans. Publicly interrogated by the members of the civic leagues, he replied to them without concealment.

"You ask me what I think of our political system, of our committees, and their leaders. I have made it my business for years to observe and understand that system, and I hate it as thoroughly as I understand it. You are quite right in saying that the system is bi-partisan; that it constitutes 'the most dangerous condition in the public life of our State and nation to-day'; and that it has virtually, for the time being, 'destroyed representative government, and put in its place a government of privilege.' I would propose to abolish it by the above reforms, by the election to office of men who will refuse to submit to it, and bend all their energies to break it up, and by pitiless publicity."

He was asked what his relations would be with his own party managers. He replied: "I would consider, if I am elected, that I am myself the head of my party, and the direct representative of the whole people in the conduct of the government."

Mr. Wilson was elected. He had a majority of 50,000 votes, replacing a Republican who had been elected with a majority of 80,000. His campaign had displaced and gained 130,-000 votes. The elections to the legislature, which had taken place at the same time, had equally favoured the democratic party to which he belonged. The republican majority of 31 on a joint ballot had now become a democratic majority of 21. Nothing more remained for Mr. Wilson but to prove his authority and govern as he had promised.

He did not fail. He had to fight, but the battle was short and decisive. We have already referred to James Smith, the local politician and "boss," who retired in favour of Mr. Wilson. Mr. Wilson had in fact exacted his resignation. In the convention which had

proclaimed his candidature, names had been
discussed for one of the two senatorial seats
which belonged to the State of New Jersey in
the federal Senate of the United States. Mr.
Wilson had requested that James Smith should
not be nominated, as he did not wish his name
associated with that of the "boss." His demand was admitted. A certain James E. Martine was selected in the place of Smith, and
Mr. Wilson believed the matter settled by this
resignation and selection. He was deceived.
With indignation he learned that James
Smith's resignation was simply a trick. On
the morrow of the electoral success Smith tran-
quilly declared that there had been a mistake,
that he had recovered from the illness which
had attacked him, and that he was the candidate and not Mr. Martine. His political
friends did not contradict these assertions.

For an instant Mr. Wilson was surprised by
the cynicism of the ruse, and by the clumsy re-
erection of the political machine he had promised to control. But he understood that he
must from that moment either gain or lose his
party. The position was very difficult. The senator, representative of New Jersey at Washington, was elected not by universal suffrage
but by the electoral body, the state legislature
constituted by members of both Houses, the

politicians who had been accustomed to march with and follow their "bosses." Mr. Wilson thus found himself surrounded by his adversaries, and in grave danger of being rapidly and definitely humiliated. The combat was unavoidable, and he accepted the challenge. He first addressed himself to James Smith, reminded him of his promise, and called upon him to keep it. Mr. James Smith paid no attention to the demand, and Mr. Wilson immediately addressed himself to the people.

"I realise the delicacy of taking any part in the discussion of the matter [he said]. As Governor of New Jersey I shall have no part in the choice of Senator. Legally speaking, it is not my duty even to give advice with regard to the choice. But there are other duties besides legal duties. The recent campaign has put me in an unusual position. I offered, if elected, to be the political spokesman and advisor of the people. I even asked the voters who did not care to make their choice of governor upon that understanding not to vote for me. I believe that the choice was made upon that understanding and I cannot escape the responsibility involved. I have no desire to escape it. It is my duty to say, with a full sense of the peculiar responsibility of my position, *what I*

*deem to be the obligation of the legislature to
do in this gravely important matter."*

We have italicized these words. They express the whole sense and essence of what may
be called the Wilsonian revolution, a revolution long meditated and pre-meditated, for we
have found its definition in the earliest works
of our author. He had always desired what
he was able to do that day, to bring together
Executive and Legislative, artificially separated by the written constitution of the United
States, to create an authority—a personal authority—which imposed its will upon the two
Houses, advising them, leading them, and governing them, and telling them *what it considered should be their duty in serious cases.* We
recall the origin because it is that origin which
gives significance to the local incident. Trace
a straight line from the origin to this episode,
continue the line by an imaginary prolongation. This prolongation will show at a not
very remote point a great fact. In March,
1917, President Wilson told his people what
he considered to be their duty in the gravest of
circumstances, and he launched that people into
war. But let us return to this State Governorship in which Mr. Wilson was beginning to
exercise himself and show his quality.

He had satisfaction of the "boss" who had tried to trick him. Smith was definitely rejected and Martine elected senator. This first victory cleared the ground, and rendered almost easy those which followed. Mr. Wilson took the direction of the legislative work. The constitution of the State of New Jersey enacts that the Governor "should communicate with the Houses by means of a message at the commencement of each session, and at such other times as he should deem necessary, recommending to them such measures as he considered advisable." This written law produced feeble results. Mr. Wilson armed himself with the text, and gave fresh life to the function. Addressing himself to the members, he told them what he expected from them in the name of public opinion. The constitution did not authorise him to participate in the legislative debates, and he had to abstain from them. But he participated in the meetings of the democratic party of which he considered himself the leader at the same time as Governor of the State. He was not invited to participate. He invited himself, asserting himself, and speaking with a tenacity and authority which tired his adversaries.

Governor Wilson's legislative work is of high interest. But the French reader would

not be likely to understand it without previous
explanation.   The atmosphere and the problems have no analogies in France.   Our institutions have numerous defects, but they cannot be compared with American institutions as
their character is so different.   If we wish to
understand the politics of the United States of
America we must remember that this immense
nation of mixed race—illiterates, streaked with
Calabrian, Syrian, and Croat blood—is governed by laws set up in 1787 by English and
Scottish colonists under the guidance of a rural
aristocracy and the cream of Puritan jurists.
These men organised an ingenious and complicated system of officials elected to arbitrate
upon the difficulties which cropped up.   They
took for granted that these difficulties would
be exceptional and trifling, for their activities
were dispersed across the vast scattered space
in which they lived.   They thought, and not
without reason, that these officials could not
be very numerous.   So they decided to name
them—judges, administrators, militia officers,
school directors—by the selection of the ballot.
The old colonists in this way almost succeeded
in suppressing the State and establishing a free
republic.   The reality is remote, the survivals
are absurd.   An Americanised Bulgarian who
can scarcely speak English, who cannot write,

can nominate, in other words can select each year, if he lives in a large town, a hundred officials. Illiterate himself he can yet turn the wheels of the most difficult political machinery. His incapacity is conspicuous. This unhappy person must not be crushed, for if he is incapable no one is capable. The most clear-headed and careful citizen of an American city is overwhelmed by the duties thrust upon him by an old-fashioned constitution, by the number and frequency of the choice demanded from him. Thus arises the power of the committee and the politician, the "machines" and the "bosses." They are the specialists who fabricate the lists and manipulate the ballots exactly as merchants buy their goods and make a market. Mr. Wilson touched upon the subject with some force a few months before his election in March, 1909, when addressing one of the civic leagues which devote themselves to studying these problems.

"You have given the people of this country so many persons to select for office that they have not time to select them, and have to leave it to professionals, that is to say, the professional politicians; which, reduced to its simplest term, is the boss of the district. When you vote the republican or democratic ticket you either vote for the names selected by one machine or the names selected by the other machine. This is not to lay any aspersion upon those who receive the nominations. I for one do not subscribe to the opinion that bosses under our Government deserve our scorn and contempt, for we have organised a system of government which makes them just as necessary as the President of the United States. They are the natural, inevitable fruit of the tree, and if we do not like them we have got to plant another tree. The boss is just as legitimate as any member of any legislature, because by giving the people a task which they cannot perform, you have taken it away from them, and have made it necessary that those who can perform it should perform it. . . ."

Under a final analysis the constitution proves faulty because it is fictitious, and fictitious because it is out of date. Being obsolete, necessarily it must disappear before occult but energetic and actual force. Mr. Wilson dealt also with this aspect.

"What is the moral? I have already said it, and said it again, to the students at my lectures. To-day, for the first time, I offer it to my fellow citizens in conference assembled outside the confines of the college. I have for a long while deferred the task which appeared at first discouraging. The remedy is con-

tained in one word, *Simplification*. Simplify
your processes, and you will begin to control;
complicate them, and you will get farther and
farther away from their control.

"Simplification! Simplification! Simplification! is the task that awaits us: to reduce the
number of persons voted for to the absolute
workable minimum,—knowing whom you have
selected; knowing whom you have trusted, and
having so few persons to watch that you can
watch them. That is the way we are going to
get popular control back in this country, and
that is the only way we are going to get popular control back. . . . Act in any other manner—name, for example, new officials expressly charged to watch those you have already elected, and you will have obtained nothing but a new weakness in your control."

Simplification; in other words to level to the
intelligence of the multitude a constitution
based upon the political intelligence of a patri-
archal and highly cultivated society. Simplification; to shape to the needs of a modern
state, weighted with enterprises and responsibilities, a constitution planned for the needs
of a primitive state, to arbitrate between the
citizens rather than to lead the people. Simplification of electoral procedure, of the mechanism of control, of the concentration of power.

To form from the elements of a republican society, founded by eighteenth century Puritan
colonists, a new, authoritative and popular society, Cæsarian in more than one respect.
This was the task Mr. Wilson defined so
clearly, a task he attempted within the limited
scope of his powers.

At first he wished to reduce the secret influences. He wanted to secure the control of the
political and financial combinations which governed under the pretence of a fictitious democracy. He favoured the passing of a law insisting upon the publicity of conventions and
the deliberations of the Parties, and regulat-
ing the methods by which they selected the
candidates. There was a lively resistance.
Dissenting Democrats united with Republicans
in concerted opposition to defeat the bill. At
this meeting to which he had not been asked
Governor Wilson arrived self-invited. He
spoke for four hours. Overcoming his opponents, he secured the necessary support. The
law was passed. On one hand it increased
the power of the people, on the other the power
of the Governor, at the expense of these secret
committees of the Parties. The Governor was
given a legal right to assist at those party con-
ferences which decided upon the programmes.
This innovation was actively attacked on the

ground that the Governor would become a dictator. "This is really a powerful argument in its favour. We have outgrown the notion that the concentration of power necessarily means tyranny. The course we ought to pursue is the adoption of means for securing the location of power in the hands of the most responsible authority." *

Mr. Wilson then occupied himself with the financial bodies dealing with the public services. They are numerous in the United States, where the municipalities do not usually undertake such enterprises as the supply of their own gas, water, and traction. They are powerful, and constantly intrigue amongst the representatives and parties, seeking friends, secretly by bribery, publicly by "propaganda" subventions. Mr. Wilson resolved to end this traffic by suppressing all relationship between the industrial combinations and the members of the legislature. He introduced into the State of which he was governor a measure already passed by other states. He created an administrative commission of public services, a Public Utilities Commission. The purpose of this institution, according to an American

*The New Stateism, by John M. Mathews, in the North American Review, for June, 1911.

writer,* was "to divorce all corporate regulation from politics by taking it out of the hands
of the Legislature and placing it in the control of a small administrative body." Four
members sat upon this body, with jurisdiction
over water, gas, telephone, tramway, railway
and other companies. They had power to in-
vestigate the actions of these companies, their
formation, and their financial conditions. The
responsibility of a few competent and well re-
munerated men was substituted for that of
some hundreds of elected representatives.

Mr. Wilson did not rest until he had finished
all the reforms inscribed on his programme.
Public opinion gave him powerful assistance.
The Legislature could resist no longer. The
laws of the State of New Jersey imposed many
meetings upon the municipalities, elected more
officials than representatives, and all equally
dependent upon the Parties. Mr. Wilson
modified this legal framework and gave it
greater pliancy. New laws were passed au-
thorising the municipalities to govern themselves according to a more modern view, in
the shape of commissions elected by direct
popular vote and presided over by a salaried
mayor. Twenty-four cities, including Jersey

* Young: "The New American Government and Its Work,"
chap. xviii.

City, Atlantic City, Trenton, and Hoboken, soon took advantage of this arrangement.

This was not all. Laws were passed which repressed electoral corruption, also a law which determined the responsibility of masters in respect to workmen's accidents. . . . He obtained these results in the short space of a year; he succeeded in carrying them through by his energy, his persistence, and his extraordinary good luck.

Other reforms were meditated. The constitution forbade him to take part in legislative debates. Like our French President, he was kept apart from them. Mr. Wilson wished to have this rule modified, and so increase the power of his intervention. But a rude reversal of fortune troubled his activity. A notable section of the Democrats declared itself against him, and became allied with the Republicans, thus securing a majority in the Senate and Assembly in November, 1911. From that date Mr. Wilson's government was exercised with difficulty. He succeeded, however, in having passed into law an important bill which placed the financial companies under an exact control. This ended scandals already referred to. Business men hunted out of New York were no longer able to cross the Hudson and continue their traffic at Hoboken or Jersey City.

Mr. Wilson had done enough to prove his capacity. "Mr. Wilson's five months' record [wrote a Canadian journalist] has shown that he is an idealist who can down the politicians and get results."

V—*The First Presidential Candidature*

IN addition to these activities Mr. Wilson was able to employ his thoughts other than in the government of his State. The presidential election of 1912 was drawing near. In June the Parties would select their candidates, and in November the people would cast their vote. In 1911 Mr. Wilson made a tour from one political conference to another, even going so far as the states bordering the Pacific. In January, 1912, he delivered a speech at Washington which placed him in the front rank of his party. He was ready, and not to be ignored.

A word must be said in explanation of these American Parties, so different from the French, and at first so difficult to understand. Our parties have systematic programmes upon which their debates are based. When we think of the two famous American parties, the Republicans and the Democrats, our first and very natural idea is to seek the difference between their programmes. But this difference is hard to find, which surprises and troubles us. Without question at one time some difference existed. The Republicans were in favour of a centralised and developed power. The Democrats preferred the autonomy of the states. The opposite tendencies produced in 1861 a sanguinary crisis, a civil war between the autonomist South and the more unified North. Half-a-century has passed, and the question which led the two parties into battle has lost its sharpness, and exists no longer. Another and more constant question divides them. The Republicans are protectionist, whilst the Democrats incline towards free trade. This, however, is but a tendency, and not sufficient in itself to explain the existence of two formidable organisations deeply rooted in the smallest of towns. Might we say that the democratic party is more "advanced" than its rival? It can be said. Bryan, to some extent the Jaurès of the United States, is one of the leaders. The high finance of New York, at Wall Street, supports the republican party. But to these deductions it would be easy to offer opposing indications. The democratic party has also financiers to support it. The Republicans include leaders of sections which vigorously denounce the trusts. If Bryan is fought by conservative Republicans he is no less opposed by democratic Conservatives, the Democrats of the Southern States. Mr. Wilson must actually be included amongst them. He has never dissimulated the aversion inspired in him by the demagogic compliances of his political associate Bryan. When, for the first time, in 1906, he considered a presidential candidature, he sought for the support of the democratic Conservatives. But these general observations do not greatly advance our enquiry, and the question remains almost unanswered. Why a republican party? Why a democratic party? And why are the two parties irreducibly opposed? The reply undoubtedly is that they exist because at some former time they had a reason to exist, that they continue to exist because they have become veritable institutions, societies for political advancement, administrative enterprises with a following. These two parties have been compared to the two great Parisian stores, the Louvre and the Bon Marché. Both have the same function of supplying household goods. They rival each other in making offers, each one cheaper and more attractive than the other. There are the floating customers who give their patronage to one or the other according to the fascination of the service offered. The comparison is not inexact. A French reader will do well to fix it in his memory if he wishes to rid himself of the embarrassment of attaching

too clear and sharp a meaning to words worn
by much usage.

What was the position in 1912 of the two
Parties? The Republicans had held the Presidential office for a long while, and were fa-
tigued. Roosevelt governed from 1902 to 1908
with a noisy violence which had ceased to
please. Taft had then been elected. He had
governed honestly and skilfully, but without
brilliance. He did not captivate a country
which loves the inspiration of leadership. The
republican party supported the candidature of
a leader who had not forfeited their esteem.
Taft would have had many chances if Roosevelt had not suddenly undertaken to divide the
electorate by proposing himself as a candidate
in the name of a new party which called itself
Progressist. He presented a very fine national
and democratic programme. But it lacked
solid organisation, and a divided party gave
wonderful chances to such disciplined opponents as the Democrats. Reunited in conference in June, 1912, they struck out the candidature of Bryan, selecting as champion one
who had already given proof of knowledge,
prudence, and capacity. This man was Wilson. When declared candidate his name was
acclaimed by cheering which lasted for an hour
and a quarter. This was a good omen. It was

remembered, however, that when Bryan was selected as candidate in 1908 the cries, stampings, and bravos had continued for one hour and twenty-seven minutes.

His destiny had suddenly enlarged. Wilson was in the running for the first magistrature in the world. What figure would he cut in such a test? We have followed his career when, as a professor, he spoke with deep knowledge and wisdom. As president of a university his words were authoritative, lofty, and eloquently impressive. As Governor of a State he spoke clearly, and with the requisite force. In a word, this tenacious and supple man, eminently capable, had been to that moment equal to all the tasks he had undertaken. He had now to address himself to the multitude, and to persuade and inspire the most vast and mixed of peoples. This was a different task. Let us see how he attempted and set about it.

In France we are easily able to study his actual words. During 1913 a volume entitled "The New Freedom," containing the speeches delivered in the course of his presidential candidature, was translated and published in French. In addressing the crowd Mr. Wilson modified his language. His historic realism was slightly put on one side in the shade.

Crowds, as he well knew, are always in the depths of their being optimists and believers, and to be swayed by idealistic appeals and religious phraseology. His new style of eloquence was idealist and religious, democratic and levelling. He seemed to arrive at this effect immediately and without effort, as if he were guided in his steps by the true instinct of public life—what should be said, and the manner in which it should be said. The transformation is so striking that we cannot study the life of Mr. Wilson without endeavouring to discover the determining springs of action. In an interesting article already quoted Miss Ida Tarbell also observed the fact and was equally astonished. She asked herself the same question: "Mr. Wilson's career having been for so long that which ordinarily produces the intellectual aristocrat of America, how did he become the great Democrat he so incontestably is at the present day?" And she continues: "I asked him the question." "I do not know," he replied frankly. "I was not conscious that a change had been at work in me. Certainly my family stock and origin must be taken into account. By blood I am a mixture of Scotch and Irish. There is no true aristocracy in Scotland, neither is there any real peasantry. The only difference between one Scotchman and another is that of education. There has never been any bar between me or any one else except a difference in taste. My father was the same." This explanation must undoubtedly be kept in mind. But we must not be discouraged from seeking others. Why did this remote hereditary strain slumber so long? What could have made it so suddenly active, if it was not this instinct of public life which animates Mr. Wilson's personality, a singular instinct, at once practical and realistic, suggesting to him at every moment the most effective words. He always endeavoured to gain the approbation and the support of the audiences which listened to him. The emotion of a crowd is the most powerful force in the world. He conjured it up, and handled it with the skill of a master. "In politics," he said to Miss Ida M. Tarbell, "I am a pragmatist. My first thought is, what results will be given?"

We have already noted the wise eloquence of Mr. Wilson, when, as a university professor, he recommended the study of classical tradition to his pupils. Classical learning remains a solid legacy of thirty centuries of experience to a humble present and an always uncertain future. Listen now to the voice of the other Wilson, the popular candidate for the leader-

ship of a nation. Listen as he speaks to this
American people, exalting before them, and
with them, the great innovation, and the infi-
nite hopes of American history. They are not
speeches [wrote M. Jean Izoulet, the French
translator of "The New Freedom"], they are
hymns. We do not know which to admire—
the simple and deep inspiration, or the profound religious tone.

"No matter how often we think of it, the
discovery of America must each time make a
fresh appeal to our imaginations. For centuries, indeed from the beginning, the face of
Europe had been turned toward the east. All
the routes of trade, every impulse and energy,
ran from west to east. The Atlantic lay at the
world's back-door. Then, suddenly the conquest of Constantinople by the Turk closed the
route to the Orient. Europe had either to face
about or lack any outlet for her energies; the
unknown sea at the west at last was ventured
upon, and the earth learned that it was twice
as big as it had thought. Columbus did not
find, as he had expected, the civilisation of
Cathay; he found an empty continent. In that
part of the world, upon that new-found half
of the globe, mankind, late in its history, was
thus afforded an opportunity to set up a new

civilisation; here it was strangely privileged to make a new human experiment.

"Never can that moment of unique opportunity fail to excite the emotion of all who consider its strangeness and richness; a thousand fanciful histories of earth might be contrived without the imagination daring to conceive such a romance as the hiding away of half the globe until the fulness of time had come for a new start in civilisation. A mere sea-captain's ambition to trace a new trade route gave way to a moral adventure for humanity. The race was to found a new order here on this delectable land, which no man approached without receiving, as the old voyagers relate, you remember, sweet airs out of woods aflame with flowers and murmurous with the sound of pellucid waters. The hemisphere lay waiting to be touched with life—life from the old centres of living surely, but cleansed of defilement, and cured of weariness, so as to be fit for the virgin purity of a new bride. The whole thing springs into the imagination like a wonderful vision, an exquisite marvel which once only in all history could be vouchsafed.

"One thing other only compares with it; only one other thing touches the springs of emotion as does the picture of the ships of Columbus drawing near the bright shores—that is the thought of the choke in the throat of the immigrant of to-day as he gazes from the steerage deck at the land where he has been taught to believe he in his turn shall find an earthly paradise, where, a free man, he shall forget the heartaches of the old life, and enter into the fulfilment of the hope of the world. For has not every ship that has pointed her prow westward borne hither the hopes of generation after generation of the oppressed of other lands? How always have men's hearts beat as they saw the coast of America rise to their view! How it has always seemed to them that the dweller there would at last be rid of kings, of privileged classes, and of all those bonds which had kept men depressed and helpless, and would there realise the full fruition of his sense of honest manhood, would there be one of a great body of brothers, not seeking to defraud and deceive one another, but seeking to accomplish the general good!

"What was in the writings of the men who founded America? To serve the selfish interests of America? Do you find that in their writings? No; to serve the cause of humanity, to bring liberty to mankind. They set up their standards here in America in the tenet of hope, as a beacon of encouragement to all the nations of the world; and men came thronging to these shores with an expectancy that never existed before, with a confidence they never dared feel before, and found here for generations together a haven of peace, of opportunity, of equality.

"God send that in the complicated state of modern affairs we may recover the standards and repeat the achievements of that heroic age!"

Let us recover our standards, he said, for they have been lost. America is "in a fair way of failure—tragic failure," menaced by a new form of slavery which must be fought by a new freedom. Who are the masters attempting to dominate the country? They are the great financiers, the Magnates who corrupt the Parties, who through the Parties grip the Congress and through the Congress paralyse the President, the direct agent of the People. Energetic action must be taken against them. "It may be too late to turn back."

What can be done? * The healthy and open alliance existing between the President and the People must be so organised as to dissolve the secret and unwholesome connivance of Magnates and Congress. The President must be

*Cf. M. Jean Lzoulet's introduction to "La Nouvelle Liberté," p. 16.

freed. "The idea of the Presidents we have recently had has been that they were Presidents of a National Board of Trustees. That is not my idea. I have been President of one board of trustees, and I do not care to have another on my hands. I want to be President of the people of the United States." The nation must be freed and the constitution modified, or trouble would follow. Three new powers were necessary. There must be the right of *Referendum,* that is to say the right to reject at need any law the Congress may seek to impose. This in itself is not sufficient. There must be the right of *Initiative,* the inverse right to impose upon Congress any law Congress may wish to elude. To these double powers of *Initiative* and *Referendum* must be added the third power of *Revocation,* the power of revoking, according to certain definite procedure, administrative officials.

"Let no man be deceived by the cry that somebody is proposing to substitute direct legislation by the people, or the direct reference of laws passed in the legislature to the vote of the people, for representative government. The advocates of these reforms have always declared, and declared in unmistakable terms, that they were intending to recover representative government, not supersede it; that the

initiative and referendum would find no use in
places where legislatures were really representative of the people whom they were elected
to serve. The initiative is a means of seeing
to it that measures which the people want shall
be passed—when legislatures defy or ignore
public opinion. The referendum is a means of
seeing to it that the unrepresentative measures
which they do not want shall not be placed upon
the statute book.

"When you come to the recall, the principle
is that if an administrative officer—for we will
begin with the administrative officer—is corrupt or so unwise as to be doing things that are
likely to lead to all sorts of mischief, it will be
possible by a deliberate process prescribed by
the law to get rid of that officer before the end
of his term. You must admit that it is a little
inconvenient sometimes to have what has been
called an astronomical system of government,
in which you can't change anything until there
has been a certain number of revolutions of
the season. In many of our oldest states the
ordinary administrative term is a single year.
The people of those states have not been willing
to trust an official out of their sight more than
twelve months. Elections there are a sort of
continuous performance, based on the idea of
the constant touch of the hand of the people on

their own affairs. That is exactly the principle of the recall. I don't see how any man grounded in the traditions of American affairs can find any valid objection to the recall of administrative officers. The meaning of the recall is this—not that we should have unstable government, not that officials should not know how long their power might last—but that we might have government exercised by officials who know whence their power came and that if they yield to private influences they will presently be displaced by public influences.

"You will of course understand that, both in the case of the initiative and referendum and in that of the recall, the very existence of these institutions, the very possibilities which they imply, are half—indeed, much more than half —the battle. They rarely need to be actually exercised. The fact that the people may initiate keeps the members of the legislature awake to the necessity of initiating themselves; the fact that the people have the right to demand the submission of a legislative measure to popular vote renders the members of the legislature wary of bills that would not pass the people; the very possibility of being recalled puts the official on his best behaviour."

President and People being thus strengthened and in unison must employ their force to reduce the power of the "Magnates." How can it be diminished? By the reform of the protectionist tariff, the reform of the banking system, the establishment of public control of all trusts. The reform of the protectionist tariff would come first.

"Under the high tariff there has been formed a network of factories, which in their connection dominate the market of the United States and establish their own prices. Whereas, therefore, it was once arguable that the high tariff did not create the high cost of living, it is now no longer arguable that these combinations do not—not by reason of the tariff, but by reason of their combination under the tariff —settle what prices shall be paid; settle how much the product shall be; and settle what shall be the market for labour.

"The 'protective' policy, as we hear it proclaimed to-day, bears no relation to the original doctrine enunciated by Webster and Clay. The 'infant industries,' which those statesmen desired to encourage, have grown up and grown grey, but they have always had new arguments for special favours. Their demands have gone far beyond what they dared ask for in the days of Mr. Blaine and Mr. McKinley, though both those apostles of 'protection' were, before they died, ready to confess that the time had even then come to call a halt on the claims of the subsidised industries. William McKinley, before he died, showed symptoms of adjustment to the new age such as his successors have not exhibited. You remember how he joined in opinion with what Mr. Blaine before him had said; namely, that we had devoted the country to a policy which, too rigidly persisted in, was proving a policy of restriction; and that we must look forward to a time that ought to come very soon when we should enter into reciprocal relations of trade with all the countries of the world. This was another way of saying that we must substitute elasticity for rigidity; that we must substitute trade for closed ports. McKinley saw what his successors did not see. He saw that we had made for ourselves a strait-jacket.

". . . We mean that our tariff legislation henceforth shall have as its object, not private profit, but the general public development and benefit; we shall make our fiscal laws, not like those who dole out favours, but like those who serve a nation. We are going to begin with those particular items where we find special privilege entrenched. We know what those items are; these gentlemen have been kind enough to point them out themselves. What

we are interested in first of all with regard to
the tariff is getting the grip of special interests off the throat of Congress. We do not
propose that special interests shall any longer
camp in the rooms of the Committee on Ways
and Means of the House and the Finance
Committee of the Senate. We mean that those
shall be places where the people of the United
States shall come and be represented, in order
that everything may be done in the general
interest, and not in the interest of particular
groups of persons who already dominate the
industries and the industrial development of
this country. Because, no matter how wise
these gentlemen may be, no matter how patriotic, no matter how singularly they may be
gifted with the power to divine the right
courses of business, there isn't any group of
men in the United States, or in any other country, that is wise enough to have the destinies
of a great people put into their hands as trustees. We mean that business in this land shall
be released, emancipated.

"Afterwards, by the revision of the banking
system, the power of the Magnates could be attacked. The banking system was old-fashioned, out of date, and bad in every respect.
The Magnates allowed it to continue because
they knew that on the day of reformation the

federal state would insist upon becoming an associated manager in the administration of national monetary reserves. The moment for this reform could not be delayed. The Magnates must become accustomed to the idea that the public has the right to see clearly into their business. They must resign themselves to the necessity of opening their books and submitting their documents to the State Commissioners.

"A modern joint stock corporation is a segment of the public; bears no analogy to a partnership or to the processes by which private property is safeguarded and managed, and should not be suffered to afford any covert whatever to those who are managing it. Its management is of public and general concern, is in a very proper sense everybody's business. The business of many of these corporations which we call public-service corporations, and which are indispensable to our daily lives and serve us with transportation and light and water and power,—their business, for instance, is public business; and, therefore, we can and must penetrate their affairs by the light of examination and discussion.

"In New Jersey, the people have realised this for a long time, and a year or two ago we got our ideas on the subject enacted into legislation. The corporations involved opposed the legislation with all their might. They talked about ruin—and I really believe they did think they would be somewhat injured. But they have not been. And I hear I cannot tell you how many men in New Jersey say, 'Governor, we were opposed to you; we did not believe in the things you wanted to do, but now that you have done them, we take off our hats. That was the thing to do, it did not hurt us a bit; it just put us on a normal footing; it took away suspicion from our business.' New Jersey, having taken the cold plunge, cries out to the rest of the states, 'Come on in! The water's fine!' I wonder whether these men who are controlling the government of the United States realise how they are creating every year a thickening atmosphere of suspicion, in which presently they will find that business cannot breathe.

"So I take it to be a necessity of the hour to open up all the processes of politics and of public business—open them wide to public view; to make them accessible to every force that moves, every opinion that prevails in the thought of the people; to give society command of its own economic life again, not by revolutionary measures, but by a steady application of the principle that the people have a right to look into such matters and to control them; to cut all privileges and patronage and private advantage and secret enjoyment out of legislation.

"Wherever any public business is transacted, wherever plans affecting the public are laid, or enterprises touching the public welfare, comfort and convenience go forward, wherever political programmes are formulated, or candidates agreed on—over that place a voice must speak, with the divine prerogative of a people's will, the words: 'Let there be light!'"

Such, in their main lines, were the politics of the candidate Wilson. It was not a conservative policy. Supported by a popular enthusiasm, which was directly excited, it kept in sight and aimed at constitutional modifications. It was not a revolutionary policy. It desired the reinforcement of the powers of the state, and the subordination of the parts to the whole. It was at once a popular and authoritative policy which we may call Cæsarian. Mr. Wilson entitled the collection of speeches made during the electoral campaign "The New Freedom." The qualification is prudent, for the freedom he promised was assuredly new, and a nineteenth-century Liberal would hardly recognise it. "Human freedom," he said in one

of his addresses, "consists in perfect adjustment of human interests and human activities
and human energies to one another." This
interlocking has no relationship with that quest
for independence of thought and life which
formed the old liberalism. Mr. Wilson knew
this, and was not frightened. This man, passionate in his desire for action, belongs without reserve to his time. And this age, as he
recognised, is not for the individual but for the
mass. When the life of the whole mass is assured, and when their elected control governs
with their unbroken consent, then, according
to Mr. Wilson, liberty is being enjoyed.

"What is liberty?" he asked again. "You
say of the locomotive that it runs free. What
do you mean? You mean that its parts are so
assembled and adjusted that friction is reduced
to a minimum, and that it has perfect adjustment. We say of a boat skimming the water
with light foot, 'How free she runs,' when
we mean, how perfectly she is adjusted to the
force of the wind, how perfectly she obeys the
great breath out of the heavens that fills her
sails. Throw her head up into the wind and
see how she will halt and stagger, how every
sheet will shiver and her whole frame be
shaken, how instantly she is 'in irons,' in the
expressive phrase of the sea. She is free only

when you have let her fall off again and have
recovered once more her nice adjustment to the
forces she must obey and cannot defy."

The concentration of power, and the unani-
mous consent of the populace,—this is what
President Wilson calls "liberty."

We must not forget that the word liberty
has other meanings. However, this political
idea, as he expressed it, is human and generous
enough, if not strictly liberal. Such a policy
is always attentive to the feelings of the people,
and always endeavours to seek their consent
and to obtain their response.

Would Mr. Wilson be elected? He had the
disadvantage of standing as the candidate of
a party which had been defeated for fifteen
years, a party which had lost the habit of victory. He had the advantage of being opposed
by a victorious party which had been worn by
its victories. The republican party, so proud
of its power, had been split by a schism. The
conservatives broke away from the progressives, the first voting for Taft, the second for
Roosevelt. Taft had the benefit of the old
party organisation, Roosevelt the enjoyment of
his personal strength and immense popularity.
He fought for a programme very similar to
that of Governor Wilson. But he was sup-

ported by partisans rather than by a party, and
that spoilt his chances.

The American presidential election is divided into two parts. The original idea of the
founders of the constitution was to take from
the mass its initiative of choice and to hand
it over entirely to a body of chosen delegates.
Each state named a certain number of delegates proportionate to the figure of its population, down to a minimum of three, which
could not be further reduced. New York
State, for example, possesses forty-five votes,
Pennsylvania thirty-eight, Delaware, Nevada,
and Wyoming, three each. The process takes
a long time, but practice has disappointed the
intentions of the drafters of the constitution.
The political parties and the people very quickly
reaffirmed their power, the parties by selecting
long in advance their presidential candidates,
the people by imposing on the delegates their
imperative mandate for one candidate or the
other. A choice is made between two or three
candidates proposed by the parties. In each
State the delegates vote, and the vote of the entire State is given to the successful candidate.
The system is rudimentary, and minorities are
wiped out. The result is that in New York
State a majority of eleven hundred votes gives
the casting vote in an electoral body of more

than a million electors, determines the election of thirty-six decocratic delegates, and wipes out the views of a republican minority consisting of more than forty-nine per cent of the electorate. The system can even overcome a majority. Let us imagine three lists of delegates proposed to the electoral body. One obtains six, another four, a third three, total thirteen. That will give seven divided against six massed. The six have the advantage that their votes will represent the thirteen. These facts must be remembered to understand Mr. Wilson's first election. He was elected although he had not the majority of the popular vote. This can be seen in the figures.

	Delegate Votes	Popular Votes
Wilson	435	6,286,087
Roosevelt	88	4,125,804
Taft	8	3,475,813
Debs (socialist)	0	895,892
Chafin (prohibitionist)	0	200,772
Reinur (labour)	0	38,814

Thus Mr. Wilson, having obtained 6,286,-087 votes against 8,737,295, that is to say, being in a minority of 2,450,308 votes, was elected the supreme head of the people of the United States.

VI—*The Presidency: Reforms*

WHAT kind of a President was the country about to have? Mr. Taft had been a prudent and conservative head of the state. He had administered public affairs in the manner of a scientific and peaceful jurist. Mr. Wilson's past was in itself a clear warning that he would act in quite a different way. Would he be a new Roosevelt? The two men were far from alike—one bubbling over with words, exuberant, a sort of Niagara, the other a being of ice, a living enigma. "The elongated features, from forehead to the large and slightly projecting chin, mark tenacity and stubbornness," wrote an excellent French observer, M. Lechartier, in the *Journal des Débats,* April 19, 1916. "The thin lips, with their vague bitterness and sense of disallusion, in their very smile add a sarcasm to his words. His looks, generally fixed on the ground, though soft, express fatigue or an unutterable weariness. His voice is musical, and rather deeper than the ordinary. In public and open air speaking it gathers strength but never warmth. His ges-

tures are generally very restrained, but in front
of an audience, from a platform, they become
amplified and automatically sweeping and
jerky, punctuating and marking his thoughts
so academically and magnificently expressed.
In attitude, manner, and appearance he appears to keep a constant watch upon himself.
His height apparently increased because he is
thin, the President of the United States gives
at first sight a very strong impression of reserve, self-control, and coldness. This impression becomes stronger at each meeting, and
it certainly becomes extremely difficult to penetrate this chilliness, and to know the personality of the President of the United States."

How Mr. Wilson was going to govern was
not known. But one thing was sure. He
would govern. His inaugural address, delivered in March, 1913, was very lofty in tone.
The moving peroration, read in the light of to-
day's knowledge, appears startling.

"The feelings with which we face this new
age of right and opportunity sweep across our
heart strings like some air out of God's own
presence, where justice and mercy are reconciled and the judge and the brother are one.
We know our task to be no mere task of politics, but a task which shall search us through
and through, whether we be able to understand

our time and the need of our people, whether
we be indeed their spokesmen and interpreters,
whether we have the pure heart to compre-
hend and the rectified will to choose our high
course of action.   This is not a day of tri-
umph; it is a day of dedication.   Here muster,
not the forces of party, but the forces of humanity.   Men's hearts wait upon us; men's
lives hang in the balance; men's hopes call upon
us to say what we will do.   Who shall live up
to the great trust?   Who dares fail to try?   I
summon all honest men, all patriotic, all forward-looking men, to my side.   God helping
me, I will not fail them, if they will but counsel and sustain me."

Soon appeared an indication of the line he
was likely to take, a small thing in appearance
but of great signification.   The American
Presidents have the prerogative of naming—
either alone or with the assent of the Senate
—a large number of administrative officials.
This prerogative is nevertheless an extremely
absorbing and heavy charge.   "The mere task
of making appointments to office, which the
constitution imposes upon the President [wrote
Mr. Wilson in *Constitutional Government in
the United States*] has come near to breaking
some of our Presidents down, because it is a
never-ending task in a civil service not yet put

upon a professional footing, confused with short terms of office, always forming and dissolving." Overwhelming as was this prerogative, the Presidents had always been jealous to retain its exercise because of the powerful personal influence it placed in their hands. President Wilson decided to hand the privilege over to his Secretaries of State. He announced that he would delegate his powers of nomination for each administrative department to the chief of that department. His intention was to devote the whole of his time to the governing of the state. The publication of this radical decision made an impression, and gave the President an added respect.

This early sign of his will was soon followed by a more startling manifestation. In his juvenile essay upon cabinet government, when examining for the first time the political conditions of his country, it will be remembered that he asked for more concentration and unity in the sources of power. "The executive has constantly need of the co-operation of the legislative," he wrote. "The Legislature should be assisted by an Executive capable of intelligently and vigorously carrying out its acts." Thus President Wilson expressed himself in 1879. In April, 1913, he acted. The act of the man was an exact confirmation of the youth's thoughts. The act in itself was simple. President Wilson announced that instead of forwarding a written Message to Congress he would attend in person and read his Message.

Amongst the politicians emotion was extreme. That the President had the right was certain. The constitution expressly gave it. The two first elected Presidents, Washington and John Adams, had always spoken to Congress when they had something to say. But their successor, Jefferson, who was an indifferent orator and a democratically-minded enemy of the very appearance of power, had abandoned a privilege no successor had resumed. Not a single president since November 22, 1800, had entered Congress. One hundred and thirteen years is almost long enough for the loss of a right by prescription. The politicians were stupefied. Some wished to resist. On April 7, eve of the day fixed by President Wilson for the solemnity, at a preparatory meeting two senators expressed their regrets and objections. The custom was primitive and obsolete; its restoration contrary to the spirit of the American constitution. Their colleagues listened with attention. But what could they do? The President had a support stronger even than right. He had the assent

of the public and of the masses. Some said
with a frown, "the President in Congress? A
speech from the throne!" People who heard
these remarks laughed and passed on. The
senators accepted the position with resignation,
and did not put up a resistance for which all
support was lacking.

On April 8 the President came to the House
of Representatives. The senators preceded
him to the chamber, marching two by two, and
led by Mr. Marshall, Vice-President of the Republic.

"Senators and Representatives," announced
Speaker Clark, "I have the honour to present
the President of the United States."

President Wilson rose and spoke. His first
words were a familiar and simple explanation
of his presence.

"I am very happy that the occasion has been
given me to speak directly to the two Houses
and to verify for myself the impression that
the President of the United States is not a mere
department of the Government, hailing Congress from some isolated island of jealous authority, and sending messages instead of speaking naturally and with his own voice. I am
happy to show at last that he is a human being, trying to co-operate with other human be-
ings in a common service. This experience is

pleasing to me. And in future, in the relationship we will have together, it will be the normal one."

A serious innovation was thus introduced methodically and skilfully. His manner was successful and pleased. The President then read his message. He indicated with precision the urgency of tariff reform and the principles which should guide it. "It is plain what those principles must be. We must abolish everything that bears even the semblance of privilege or of any kind of artificial advantage, and put our business men and producers under the stimulation of a constant necessity to be efficient, economical and enterprising masters of competitive supremacy, better workers and merchants than any in the world."

The next day the President again attended Congress, and in the Presidential cabinet, until then so rarely occupied, he discussed with the chairmen of committees and the leaders of the groups the immediate preparation of a scheme of tariff reform.

Such discussions are always difficult. President Wilson had perfectly analysed their secret mechanism in a study published in the *North American Review* for October, 1909.

"The methods by which tariff bills are con-

structed have now become all too familiar and
throw a significant light on the character of the
legislation involved.   Debate in the Houses has
little or nothing to do with it.   The process
by which such a bill is made is private not public, because the reasons which underlie many
of the rates imposed are private.   The
stronger faction of the Ways and Means Committee of the House makes up the preliminary
bill, with the assistance of 'experts' whom it
permits the industries most concerned to supply for its guidance.   The controlling members
of the Committee also determine what amendments, if any, shall be accepted, either from
the minority faction of the Committee, or from
the House itself.   It permits itself to be dic-
tated to, if at all, only by the imperative action of a party caucus.   The stronger faction
of the Finance Committee of the Senate, in like
fashion, frames the bill which it intends to substitute for the one sent up from the House.   It
is often to be found at work on it before any
bill reaches it from the popular chamber.   The
compromise between the two measures is arranged in private conference by conferees
drawn from the two committees.   What takes
place in the committees and in the conference
is confidential.   It is considered impertinent
for reporters to inquire.   It is admitted to be

the business of the manufacturers concerned, but not the business of the public, who are to pay the rates. The debates which the country is invited to hear in the open sessions of the Houses are merely formal. They determine nothing and disclose very little. It is the policy of silence and secrecy, indeed, with regard to the whole process that makes it absolutely inconsistent with every standard of public duty and political integrity."

This was the position in 1909, when an abortive attempt was made towards tariff reform. Upon the resumption of parliamentary labours in April, 1913, the matter took the same turn, and the intrigues of the corridors, of the "lobby" according to the phrase in the United States, were directed against the proposed measure. President Wilson was prepared for opposition, but he knew his strength and was sure to reach his aim. He was strong because tariff reform was the only reform for which the Democratic party was wholly and traditionally united. There were Democrats who were opposed to trusts or who benefited by trusts. There were democratic Democrats and also aristocratic or plutocratic Democrats. There were Northern Democrats and Southern Democrats. There were Democrats who had successively voted for the Republicans Mc-

Kinley, Roosevelt, and Taft, as well as those
who had voted with more or less enthusiasm
for Bryan. But scarcely one had ever protested against the reduction of the tariff. And,
in addition, the President was strong because
this reduction, at the moment he asked for it,
was nothing less and nothing more than a
means of fighting the power of the trusts. It
was a national necessity, the need of which
had been admitted by the Republicans when, in
1909, they had attempted the same task. The
United States had surrounded themselves with
a tariff barrier at a time when they had to pro-
tect rising industries. That was sensible.
But the question for them now was the development of powerful industries, the opening
up of world markets. The old barrier had become useless and detrimental. President Wilson's determination was sound, and he was able
to impose it without fear. He openly declared that he was in agreement with the parliamentary leaders, and that he did not seek
for, nor would he accept, any compromise.
The "lobby," however, persisted. Already the
amendments were numerous, and they threatened to equal in number the famous army of
847 which had emasculated the 1909 reform.
The President intervened in a most novel and
unexpected fashion. He published a sort of

communiqué, which was in fact an appeal to the nation.

"I think that the public ought to know the extraordinary exertions being made by the lobby in Washington to gain recognition for certain alterations of the Tariff Bill. Washington has seldom seen so numerous, so industrious, or so insidious a lobby. The newspapers are being filled with paid advertisements calculated to mislead not only the judgment of the public men, but also the public opinion of the country itself. There is every evidence that money without limit is being spent to maintain this lobby, and to create the appearance of a pressure of public opinion antagonistic to some of the chief items of the Tariff Bill.

"It is of serious interest to the country that the people at large should have no lobby, and be voiceless in these matters, while great bodies of astute men seek to create an artificial opinion and to overcome the interests of the public for their private profit. It is thoroughly worth the while of the people of this country to take knowledge of this matter. Only public opinion can check and destroy it.

"The Government in all its branches ought to be relieved of this intolerable burden and this constant interruption to the calm progress of debate. I know that in this I am speaking for the members of the two Houses, who would rejoice as much as I would to be released from this unbearable situation."

Never had a presidential document made so great an impression, never was intervention more efficacious. The "lobby" suddenly ceased, and the reform was voted.

Without loss of time another proposed reform was laid before Congress. As president of a university, as governor of a state, and here again in his new office, Mr. Wilson revealed himself as an incomparable director and stimulator of assembled bodies. He knew how to select his aims, and how to advance them by overthrowing all obstacles. This is his genius. This peculiar strength, for so long confined by the calm existence of a professorial career, presents a curious picture. And, still more singular, this public man is a very solitary man. He had always been distant in manner; he was now becoming unapproachable. He saw his secretaries of state during strictly limited interviews. Upon any particular question he preferred to receive a report rather than advice. The deponent is called, he is invited to speak, and the President listens, sometimes taking a rapid shorthand note. "I have con-

stantly remarked in the business with which I
occupy myself that there is nobody who does
not know something that I do not know, but
few who know more things than I know." He
allows then that people can instruct him, but
reserves to himself the work of synthesis. And
this man who becomes more and more solitary
also becomes more and more a man of the
crowd. He thinks with the crowd, and wishes
to become master of its thoughts. To say the
truth his one great strength is the assent of the
crowd which has elected him, listens to his messages and appeals, and which helps him to curb
the politicians by reason of the fear with which
it inspires them. This is the constant occupation of his thought. His speeches, his messages, even his diplomatic notes, are written
—and will be written—not for the crowd but
with it in his mind. The documents are always
submitted to the faithful Tumulty, his private
secretary. "Tumulty is admirable," he has
said, "for guessing the effect words may produce from the platform." If the President
lives alone, if he keeps the doors of the White
House closed, the reason is undoubtedly to be
found in his desire that the people may not sus-
pect him of intimacy with the leaders of finance,
the Magnates, to give them their American
name. They ask for interviews in vain. The

President evades or refuses their requests. Clearly he does not wish to meet them. It is a principle and an attitude, which he clings to with an increasing vigour—sometimes with harm to the general service. He interrupts his friendships of the everyday world. If he plays at golf he goes straight to the greens without passing through the clubhouse. His recreation thus becomes solitary. He is not less distant towards the politicians who wish to approach him. They insist, but obtain nothing. One of them has written a humorous complaint:

"I have seen Tumulty. I have tried that half-a-dozen times. Nothing doing. Tumulty promises, but nothing happens. Now you see I have got to go back home for several weeks. All the folks home will be asking me, 'Well, Abner, how does the President talk to you about this German business when he sees you?' So far I have bluffed them. But if they should get on to the fact that I've never seen Wilson to speak to him it would end my chance of re-election." *

On the other hand the President is extremely careful not to lose contact with the press. The press is able to manage the people. He de-

*"The Mystery of Woodrow Wilson," in the *North American Review* for September, 1917.

sires, as much as possible, to manage the press. This man, who receives nobody, devotes a special afternoon every week to a journalistic reception.   They talk to him and cross-question him upon the last diplomatic difficulty in Mexico, the tariff, or the financial problem.   Sometimes he evades the question.   "On this point my mind is not made up.   It is open."   Or, with a picturesque formula, "my mind is to let."   But he always gives an answer, and these cleverly calculated replies reach the masses through those journals the President has made the echo of his plans.

Thus he went from reform to reform.   Tariff reduction created a budget deficit.   A new tax was necessary, and federal income tax was levied.   Incomes of less than $4,000 were exempt, and incomes over that sum were taxed on a scale beginning with a minimum of one per cent.   The yield of this tax in 1913 being less than anticipated, the rates were increased in 1914.

But the most formidable enterprise in which President Wilson succeeded was the reform of the American banking system.   This system was detestable.   It was, however, acceptable to some powerful banks which had become accustomed to its defects, and were troubled at the thought of a reform which threatened to be far-reaching and also to limit their former freedom. In effect the reform did so limit them. The democratic idea was overshadowed by the power possessed by these great banks. The national interest agreed ill with institutions sheltered from control, and in certain events capable—by reason of the money they held—of influencing the state itself. The President knew how to combine the democratic idea and the national interest. Sustained by these allied forces, he resolved to recast the entire system.

"The structure of this legislation is simple," wrote Mr. H. J. Ford. "The thousands of national banks scattered throughout the country like so many separate wells were brought together into one system in which they stand as local conduits from a national reservoir. The country was divided into twelve districts, in each of which is a federal reserve bank, with which the member banks of the district keep their reserves and from which they can obtain supplies of currency on occasion by rediscount of their holdings of securities and commercial paper. Each reserve bank has its own board of directors, nine in number, six of whom are to be chosen by the member banks upon a preferential ballot scheme, and three are appointed by the Federal Reserve Board, which exercises general supervision over the system. This Board is composed of the secretary of the treasury, the comptroller of the currency, and five other members appointed by the President, and it wields such extensive powers of supervision, direction and control that it is the administrative centre of the system. There is also a body designated the Federated Advisory Council, chosen by the banks and consisting of as many members as there are federal reserve districts. The powers of this body are purely consultative, but its existence provides the banks with an organ of their own for representations to the Federal Reserve Board or for concert of action among themselves on matters of common interest. The federal reserve banks have general banking powers, and with the consent of the Federal Reserve Board may establish agencies in foreign countries. Indeed the act supplies a powerful engine for establishing the United States as a centre of international banking."

On June 23, 1913, whilst the Senate was discussing the Tariff Bill the President came to the House and spoke. He told the members that he would keep them to work despite the heat, that considerations of personal health must yield to the public good, and that it was absolutely imperative to give the country a new banking system. The representatives continued their duties without intermission. On September 9 they passed the bill which the Senate agreed to on December 19. Had it been rejected or weakened by amendments the Government of the United Staes would have been without much of that power which to-day strengthens it for the conduct of the war.

On January 20, 1914, the President addressed himself once again to Congress, demanding new legislation concerning trusts. He wished to define and to increase former restrictions. In addition he asked for the creation of a commission of enquiry and justice with sufficient powers to unravel the ramifications of the trusts and to bring them to judgment. A similar commission had already been formed to watch the railway companies. The President demanded increased powers for both. He sought to put into action one formula of his electoral campaign—to see clearly, and to obtain justice.

The President thus carried through within a single year three considerable reforms, one dealing with tariff reform, a second with the banking system, and the third with the control of trusts. This was the account of his legislative work when war broke out.

PRESIDENT WILSON needed peace to complete his legislative work. He had to deal with war. The events of August, 1914, interrupted his reforming activity.

What exactly have been President Wilson's ideas upon the subject of war? Has he ever been, according to the belief of some (and a belief not without reason), a pacifist? A knowledge of his career does not by any means help us in this respect. He has not the eloquence and military tastes of a Roosevelt. But he has studied history too well not to recognise the position and rights of war. In his history of the American people he had judged the various wars in which the United States had taken part. He had explained them, and approved of them. And he finished at last in prophesying a new America, superabundant in wealth and energy, ready to burst forth and overflow those old worlds from which she had sprung. These were not the thoughts of a pacifist.

But man proposes, and circumstances dispose. The surroundings of Mr. Wilson as candidate and president had perceptibly brought him into touch with the pacifists. The famous orator Bryan was a member of his party and a colleague and Secretary of State in his cabinet. He was obliged to make use of him. As an adversary and rival he had to meet the tumultuous Roosevelt, who was the partisan of a resolutely military and imperialistic policy. His task consisted in urging the American masses towards fresh enthusiasms, in fixing their attention upon domestic reforms which could only be brought to fruition in times of peace.

From the moment he took up office President Wilson was confronted by exterior problems and menaces of war. They multiplied across the whole face of the world. He exerted himself to remove them from his path with his customary firmness. International finance was preparing to seize the goods of China, and that nation was in urgent need of 150 millions. She was refused the sum she asked for, but offered 1,500 millions in exchange for close control and disastrous guarantees. China was about to suffer the fate of Persia and Turkey. President Wilson categorically refused to support the American financiers, and in fact insisted that they should leave the combination. This was his first step.

The administration of the Panama Canal, then in process of completion, aroused many complex and dangerous difficulties. The people of the United States were easily moved by anything affecting this great enterprise. The territory crossed by the canal belonged to Colombia. Essentially necessary to be under the control of the United States, President Roosevelt took possession of it in the most expeditious manner. Colombia protested, and, amongst other items, demanded an indemnity of ten million dollars. The South American republics interested themselves in the demand, and followed the matter with an uneasy attention. President Wilson dealt with it in the fashion of a great lord. He ended the whole business by a gift of 25 millions. As for the territory, far from giving it back he enlarged it by a slice of the Republic of Nicaragua which was useful for the security and good administration of the canal. He acquired a roadstead and its rights. He did not allow the real interests of his country to be endangered.

Another very delicate question had been unpleasantly handed to him by his predecessor Mr. Taft. Again it concerned the Panama Canal. Great Britain had discussed the subject of the canal with the United States, and had obtained a promise (which had been regularised by the Hay-Pauncefote Treaty of 1901) that the tolls levied should apply equally and without discrimination to the shipping of all nations. In exchange for this promise Great Britain professed herself disinterested in the construction and administration of the canal. But in 1912 Mr. Taft had made, or allowed, a law to pass exempting the entire coasting trade of the United States. All the European powers, in concert with Great Britain, protested. Mr. Taft refused to budge. Sir Edward Grey proposed that the difference should be carried to arbitration. The Congress had not responded and nationalist feelings were agitated. This was the position when President Wilson intervened. Assuring himself that the British demand was honest, he acted upon that ground. He went to Congress and declared that in his view "the exemption of coasting trade was in plain contravention of the Treaty of 1901. . . . We are too big and powerful and too self-respecting a nation to interpret with too strained or refined a reading of words our own promises just because we have power enough to give us leave to read them as we please. . . . The large thing to do is the only thing we can do—voluntary withdrawal from a position everywhere questioned and misunderstood." He finished in a personal and mysterious manner. "If the law is not repealed I shall not know how to deal with other matters of even greater delicacy and nearer consequence." These last words created some astonishment, and the trend of the speech made an impression. The litigious law was repealed, but not without discussion. This singular victory was gained by the President alone against the advice of both republican and democratic leaders. The date was June, 1914.

The words which had excited so much comment were explained by a further difficulty. The Mexican problem confronted President Wilson from the day he took office, and it remains still unsettled. Mexico is an immense country with great natural wealth, but poor in men capable to use it to advantage. For many miles its frontiers run with those of the United States. Formerly Austria and France coveted it. Perhaps Japan has the same ambition to-day. It remains a prey, a temptation, a trouble, and an imminent war peril. The United States have great interests in Mexico, possessing or controlling the larger industries, the railways, and the mines. In 1913 the country was in general insurrection. A nationalist party had overthrown President Diaz, accused of having over favoured the concession hunters and capitalists of the United States. The leaders of the marauding bands, Huerta and Villa, quarrelled over the government, or, more exactly, the pillage of the country and primarily the pillage of foreign property. Considerable American interests were threatened, and American citizens had been murdered. To intervene seemed legitimate and easy. In reality the question was not so simple, for it was intermingled with other problems of extreme importance. Certainly the United States were big enough to equip an army and impose it on Mexico. But behind Mexico, first republic of Latin America, were all the alarmed and vigilant South American republics. And when President Wilson faced the Mexican problem he saw in front of him another and graver problem—that of the two Americas. If he imposed his will upon Mexico he would have to do the same to the whole of Latin America, and to renounce all hopes of economic friendship or moral predominance. This would introduce into the New World all the difficulties of the Old, rivalries, alliances, diplomatic ruptures, wars. The popular press and the financial syndicates urged President Wilson towards intervention. President Taft, at the moment of giving up office, appeared to be in favour of recognising the presidency of Huerta, one of the leaders of the factions, and of protecting him as Russia protected the Shah of Persia and France the Sultan of Morocco.

Without delay President Wilson marked the change in his policy. He refused to recognise President Huerta, a brigand and assassin, declaring him unfit to govern an American state. But he said that he was prepared to recognise a president elected by constitutional methods. These friendly suggestions were not accepted, and the Mexican bands continued to kill their enemies and their associates. President Wilson followed the course of a waiting policy.

"We are happy to call ourselves the friends of Mexico," he said in his message of August 27, 1913. "It was our duty to offer our good offices for the establishment of a condition of things until a legal authority was restored in this country. . . . We have not succeeded. . . . By reason of its proximity to Mexico, the United States could not remain inactive. . . . It is now our duty to show what true neutrality will do to enable the people of Mexico to set their affairs in order again and wait for a further opportunity to offer our friendly counsels. . . . The pressure of moral force would sooner or later break down the barrier raised against us by the pride and prejudice of our neighbours. We would intervene rather as the friends of Mexico than as her enemies."

He warned his fellow citizens of the dangers they ran in remaining within the districts threatened by civil war, and also of the risks they undertook. He appeared to repudiate the imperialistic doctrine, Roman and British, which authorises a state to follow its subjects into any place and to declare war in order to defend their private interests.

The President had much to tolerate and many to conciliate. The more he endeavoured to escape this war the more it threatened him. Indifferent to his exhortations, Mexico continued its rule of brigandage, robbery, and assassination. In April, 1914, some American marines who had landed at Tampico for petrol were arrested by a Huertist colonel. The nation was attacked and insulted. Action was necessary. President Wilson moved with a rapidity and a vigour which proved that the temperament of a preaching friar was not the only foundation of his nature. He asked for full powers from Congress. They were immediately given. The President judged this sufficient, and, without waiting for the Senate to ratify the vote of the Lower House, he landed troops at Vera Cruz. The Senate protested. President Wilson explained that the occupation of Vera Cruz was not an act of war, but an act of preparation for war rendered indispensable through circumstance. . . . For several days the matter was discussed.

Was this war? Those who believed so were deceived. Once more President Wilson was able to avoid it. Argentina, Brazil, and Chili ("the A. B. C. Powers" as they are called in the New World) proposed mediation. The President admitted the proposal at once, and warmly thanked the young South American powers. Nothing could disturb his views more than the peril of a disagreement with them; nothing would satisfy him more than frank collaboration and an attempt at arbitration. The mediation was negotiated on Canadian soil at Niagara Falls. It produced no certain effect, but time had been gained, and calm had been reached. In July, Huerta, having been discredited, retired to Europe. If not peace the result was pacification, and an effective manifestation of Pan-American solidarity—in any case a gain. President Wilson was insulted by his political opponents. He paid no attention to their outrages and followed his own path. He considered, and undoubtedly not without reason, that the Republic of the

United States possessed enough real strength to be condescending without detriment to its prestige.

During the disembarkment at Vera Cruz some sailors had been killed. On May 22, 1914, President Wilson pronounced a funeral eulogy over their bodies.

"We have gone down to Mexico to serve mankind if we can find a way. We do not want to fight the Mexicans; we want to serve them if we can. A war of aggression is not a war in which it is a proud thing to die, but a war of service is one in which it is grand thing to die."

Having spoken of the dead, he had a word to say for those who had insulted him:

"I never was under fire, but I fancy there are some things just as hard to do as to go under fire. I fancy it is just as hard to do your duty when men are sneering at you as when they are shooting at you. When they shoot at you they can only take your natural life. When they sneer at you they can wound your heart. The cheers of the moment are not what a man ought to think about, but the verdict of his conscience and the conscience of mankind."

It may be thought that a funeral address is not the best means of upholding oneself, or of entering into comparison with the heroes whose memories are being exalted. But let that pass. We are now in May, 1914, at the moment when one history is ending and another beginning. Let us add the fact that President Wilson had concluded treaties of arbitration with Great Britain, France, Russia, Italy, Spain, the three Scandinavian states, China, and the greater part of the Latin republics of South America. This shows how really pacific his policy was, a more effectively peaceful policy than any chief of a state had ever yet followed. Working during a very difficult period, President Wilson had been able to elude and to send to sleep the demon of war.

Europe was struck by a thunderbolt. The first blow was in its suddenness and violence a worthy portent of the catastrophe. The peoples of Europe were surprised. Can we be astonished if it surprised the people of the New World? They learned at the same time of the menace of war, and of war itself. They could not believe in such a thing, and were still awaiting negotiations when millions of men were already in arms and at blows. Their first feeling was one of stupor. A whole world, the Old World, the womb of thought and of the arts, was streaming in blood before them. The various parts did not take shape at first.

Despondency, distress, mourning mingled with
the destruction of all hope.

We must return to the man who is the subject of our study, and who really occupies the
centre of the whole history—President Wilson.
Even in his domestic life the moment was full
of bitterness. His wife was dying, and by
her bedside he received and despatched decisive
telegrams. War had broken out. Belgium
was invaded. What was he going to do? His
responsibility was immense. The laws had
made it heavy, and tradition had increased the
load. He himself had deliberately made it
greater still, in proclaiming himself the
"leader" of his people, their director and their
chief.

What was he going to do? No one foresaw
intervention. How could the unarmed United
States intervene in a distant war which according to all judgment would be of short duration? Protestation against the violation of
Belgian neutrality was deemed vain even by
the most ardent. What was the good of pro-
testing if one was not able to act? President
Wilson must be defended against the sharp reproaches levelled at him later on by Mr. Root
and Mr. Roosevelt. Mr. Roosevelt's words
during the first weeks of the war are well
known. They express exactly the anxiety and

prudence that every neutral felt. He declared
that he would support obediently the President's policy. "I am sure that I express your
views in saying that we must first act as Americans, and that we must support every public
man who endeavours with all his force to keep
America free from this war."*

And with reference to Belgium the ex-Presi-
dent wrote: "Sympathy is compatible with
full acknowledgment of the unwisdom of our
uttering a single word of official protest unless we are prepared to make that protest effective; and only the clearest and most urgent national duty would ever justify us in deviating
from our rule of neutrality and non-inter-
vention." †

The first decisions were then relatively simple. On August 4 President Wilson issued a
declaration of neutrality. On the 5th he informed the belligerents that from that day until the end of the war he was at their service
as a mediator. On the 6th he informed all the
Powers that the Government of the United
States would watch and maintain the maritime
rights of neutrals.

There were three essential steps, but they
ended no difficulties. As a historian President

Outlook, August 15, 1914.
† *Ibid.,* September 23, 1914.

Wilson was able to remember how the United States had been dragged into the Napoleonic wars. The vigorous blockade then exercised by England on the high seas had ended in complications and war. However, in that time the United States had been a feeble power, far away and separated from the Old World. Could the new United States, so powerful and with so many interests, preserve its peace? And, if they had to fight, which should be the enemy—Germany or England? How could one guess what would take place on the high seas? There England was all powerful, and perhaps against her the United States would come into conflict. Both alternatives had to be kept in mind, and either was redoubtable. President Wilson felt that the factions forming in the United States itself were gathering force. Men of German birth or origin were deeply moved by the peril of the distant fatherland. Those who were British, and this included the entire American society of the Atlantic States, stood for France, invaded Belgium, and Great Britain. Thus the single outbreak of this distant war gravely threatened to split the unity of the young Union. No one was better able than President Wilson to measure this immense danger. The spectator who dares to disregard his anxiety and re-

proach his prudence must be rash indeed.
President Wilson knew his motley people, a
mixture of all the races of Europe—Slav, Ital-
ian, German, Jew, Polish, Irish, English. He
knew that this people, which had grown together so confusedly, remained after one hundred and thirty years the ill formed sketch of
a true race. President Wilson understood
these things to the very bottom, and was able
to gauge the imminence of a double danger, a
foreign war at the same time as a civil war.
How could he fail to feel it? The seeds of
civil war were to be found in his own person.
He was wholly English by blood, almost entirely English by education. He loved England, and from the beginning of the conflict
his sympathies were given without hesitation.
They were passionate and instinctive as well
as reflective. He had then to place them under vigorous discipline, and to give an example of the strictest and purest Americanism.
From civil war, which would be mortal, he
wished at first to turn and preserve his people. Speaking directly and paternally, on
August 18, 1914, he issued his first appeal to
the American people.

"The effect of the war upon the United
States will depend upon what American citizens say or do. Every man who really loves

America will act and speak in the true spirit of neutrality, which is the spirit of impartiality and fairness and friendliness to all concerned. The spirit of the nation in this critical matter will be determined largely by what individuals and society and those gathered in public meetings do and say, upon what newspapers and magazines contain, upon what our ministers utter in their pulpits and men proclaim as their opinions on the streets.

"The people of the United States are drawn from many nations, and chiefly from the nations now at war. It is natural and inevitable that there should be the utmost variety of sympathy and desire among them with regard to the issues and circumstances of the conflict. Some will wish one nation, others another to succeed in the momentous struggle. It will be easy to excite passion and difficult to allay it. Those responsible for exciting it will assume a heavy responsibility; responsibility for no less a thing than that the people of the United States, whose love of their country and whose loyalty to its Government should unite them as Americans all, bound in honour and affection to think first of her and her interests, may be divided into camps of hostile opinions hot against each other, involved in the war itself in impulse and opinion, if not in action. Such

divisions among us would be fatal to our peace
of mind and might seriously stand in the way
of proper performance of our duty as one great
nation at peace, the one people holding itself
ready to play a part of impartial mediation and
speak the counsels of peace and accommodation, not as a partisan but as a friend."

Peace! During those early weeks an idea
formed itself in the American mind that the
mission of the American nation was to give all
others an example of peace, and to end the war
by imposing upon the whole world a peaceful
tradition which belonged to itself alone. It
was an idea, a belief. But ideas and beliefs
are forces that President Wilson knows how
to appreciate and direct. He took up this
idea. Other leaders who wished to assure the
unity of their people have invoked blood and
race. President Wilson was not able to do
this. In the Republic of the United States the
racial spirit divides rather than unites. A material bond lacking, it was necessary to seek for
and strengthen a spiritual lien. President
Wilson made this effort, and his words became
more solemn and religious.

"I venture, therefore, my fellow-country-
men, to speak a solemn word of warning to
you against that deepest, most subtle, most essential breach of neutrality which may spring

out of partisanship, out of passionately taking sides. The United States must be neutral in fact as well as in name during these days that are to try men's souls. We must be impartial in thought as well as in action, must put a curb upon our sentiments as well as upon every transaction that might be construed as a preference of one party to the struggle before another."

He himself gave the example of the virtues he counselled. All the belligerents turned to him with their objurgations. The Emperor William telegraphed that the French did not observe the laws of war. President Poincaré telegraphed that the Germans did not observe the laws of war. King Albert protested against the violation of Belgium's rights. To all appeals the President made the same reply.

"Presently, I pray God very soon, this war will be over. The day of accounting will then come, when I take it for granted the nations of Europe will assemble to determine a settlement. Where wrongs have been committed, their consequences and the relative responsibility involved will be assessed.

"The nations of the world have fortunately by agreement made a plan for such a reckoning and settlement. What such a plan cannot compass, the opinion of mankind, the final arbiter in all such matters, will supply. It would be unwise, it would be premature, for a single government, however fortunately separated from the present struggle, it would even be inconsistent with the neutral position of any nation which, like this, has no part in the contest, to form or express a final judgment."

How vague it seems, and how chimerical! However one clear trait can be discerned, a note that persists in all the following declarations. President Wilson would not admit that the war could end in military downfall and the destruction of one of the opposed parties. He held for certain that a congress of states would settle the terms of agreement. His phraseology astonishes. It is pompous and mystical, differing strangely from the ordinary language of the chancelleries. But, in truth, President Wilson is not a diplomatist. He is the head of a popular state, and elected by the crowd. When he replies to the European governments his words must be so put together that—imprinted in the American newspapers—they are easily and usefully understood. President Wilson is always a publicist whilst being at the same time a leader. He never ceases to speak to the masses for whom he decides.

He now spoke to them with a direct solemnity he has not surpassed. He decreed that October 4 should be a day of prayer for the Republic of the United States. He brought together and taught his people with pastoral authority. This singular text, judicial and religious, must be quoted with exactness:

WHEREAS great nations of the world have taken up arms against one another and war now draws millions of men into battle whom the counsel of statesmen have not been able to save from the terrible sacrifice;

AND WHEREAS in this as in all things it is our privilege and duty to seek counsel and succour of Almighty God, humbling ourselves before Him, confessing our weakness and our lack of any wisdom equal to these things;

AND WHEREAS it is the especial wish and longing of the people of the United States, in prayer and counsel and all friendliness, to serve the cause of peace;

WHEREFORE, I, Woodrow Wilson, President of the United States of America, do designate Sunday, the fourth day of October next, a day of prayer and supplication and do request all God-fearing persons to repair on that day to their places of worship there to unite their petitions to Almighty God that, overruling the counsel of men, setting straight the things they cannot govern or alter, taking pity on the nations now in the throes of conflict, in His mercy and goodness showing a way where men can see none, He vouchsafe His children healing peace again and restore once more that concord among men and nations without which there can be neither happiness nor true friendship nor any wholesome fruit of toil or thought in the world; praying also to this end that he forgive us our sins, our ignorance of His holy will, our wilfulness and many errors, and lead us in the paths of obedience to places of vision and to thoughts and counsels that purge and make wise.

In witness whereof I have hereunto set my hand and caused the seal of the United States to be affixed.

Done at the city of Washington this eighth day of September in the year of our Lord one thousand nine hundred and fourteen and of the independence of the United States of America the one hundred and thirty-ninth.

(Seal)   WOODROW WILSON.

By the President:
    William Jennings Bryan,
        Secretary of State.

We believe this to be one of the finest pages President Wilson has written. Certainly political intentions were not wholly absent from its composition. But its thoughts are so full of grandeur, it breathes such an accent of truth and emotion, that in reading it we forget the political surroundings and wish to believe that the President himself forgot them when writing this document. He spoke. And with the voice of the Chief of the State we hear the voice of the man, the humble Woodrow Wilson, who had been hardly tried during those forty days, not only in his private life by the loss of the companion of his youth, but also in his public life by receiving on his shoulders the heaviest weight a mortal has ever carried. "But God reveals a path where men see none!" This is truly a cry of anguish. Imagine him on this

day of October 4, praying in company with his
people, bowing down in the Calvinistic temple,
his place of worship. He sees before him
darkness and danger. He collects together
his strength, his guiding principles of prudence, peace, order, and clearness of soul. He
asks the same effort of his people—passions
kept in silence, deeds restrained by discipline.

In September, the Marne. After this victory there appeared to have been an attempt
at negotiation in which President Wilson was
concerned. Was Germany beginning to recognise, without prolonging the massacre, the fu-
tility of her enterprise? The authoritative
biography of the President by Mr. Henry Jones
Ford is affirmative upon this obscure historical
point. "After the Battle of the Marne some
intimations reached him of sufficient substance
to encourage another effort and the German
Government was approached on the subject
through Ambassador Gerard at Berlin. The
Imperial Chancellor replied that as Germany's
enemies had agreed to make peace only by joint
action, the United States should obtain proposals of peace from the Allies, which must be
such as to guarantee Germany against future
attacks." There was nothing to be done. The

President allowed the negotiation to fall to the ground.

October, November, December, 1914; fighting in Flanders, fighting in Poland. People were beginning to realise that this war would be horrible in its length as well as in its violence. The Americans were always far from foreseeing or imagining their intervention. What should they do? "Let us work and give," replied and advised one of their best reviews, the *Outlook,* of December 2. "Thank God, the blessing of giving has been left to us Americans." The Americans worked and gave. They prepared convoys of food, arms, metals. They organised assistance for the wounded in northern France and Belgium, of which we shall know later the fabulous cost. They became passionately engrossed in their charitable works. They set up for their country a mission. Alone they were to continue and to safeguard the virtues of peace, thus laying the foundation for humanity's future, and becoming its arbiter by their wisdom, its guardian by their strength.

President Wilson had stood aside from public view owing to his recent mourning, the trial of circumstances, and his inborn taste for solitude whilst engaged upon the problems of his office. In every respect he favoured these moral occupations which calmed and employed the American people. He continued to give an example of pacifism. The Mexican question was still dangerous, the American troops still in occupation at Vera Cruz. The President made up his mind not to be distracted from the European menace by such secondary conflicts. He could not better gain time than in arranging this matter. Entering into negotiations with General Carranza, the most respectable of the Mexican leaders, he wished to withdraw his troops on September 16, the anniversary day of Mexican independence. This clever courtesy agreed with the spirit of his policy. He was not able to carry his wish into effect as the negotiations were still unfinished. However, on November 23, notwithstanding critics and censors, he evacuated Vera Cruz. The imperialistic party were against his action, and its opposition obliged him to seek the support of the pacifist elements. Addressing himself to this particular public, he declared himself their friend. On October 25 he spoke at a meeting of the Young Men's Christian Association:

"Your rôle is to fight, not with canon, but according to the law. We have recently concluded with a great number of powers treaties of arbitration which forbid us to break off any

negotiation without having allowed a clear year
to elapse from the date of the arbitration or
enquiry. My prediction is that a light will il-
luminate the difficulties, and that after a year
there will be no reason to fight."

He was now well engaged in a pacifist campaign, and about to go so far that his acts
would bind him. Undoubtedly his considerations were political. The legislative elections
were fixed for December, 1914, and the President had an extreme need to preserve his democratic majority. To discourage the pacifists,
to separate himself from them, could only spell
defeat. This had to be kept in mind, and he
acted in consequence. He did not forget the
example of Cleveland's presidency. Cleveland
was also a Democrat. And Cleveland had
ruined himself by coming into collision with
the democratic elements of his own party.
Like Cleveland President Wilson had the firm
resolve to govern with authority, but he was
quite decided not to be broken in the same way.

A strong section of American opinion insisted upon an increase of army and navy.
President Wilson was not in favour of such
measures. In the message of November 10 he
declared himself in fayour of "the small navy
bill" put forward by his cabinet. In Decem-

ber, 1914, in an address to Congress, he raised his voice against schemes of army reform. "We will not turn America into a camp," he said. "We will not ask our young men to spend the best years of their lives in learning soldiering." A certain league for the limitation of armaments supported his policy. He thanked it in a public reply. A man charged with such high responsibilities can only be criticised with much prudence. But it must be said that President Wilson went too far. We are able to say it more freely because he himself was soon to regret the fact, and disavowed these words. They were unfortunate because they were so unsuitable to prepare the people of the United States for an eventuality rapidly approaching.

What were President Wilson's thoughts at this moment of his presidency? What were his intentions? Did he intend to avoid war at any price? He was suspected and accused. Mr. Roosevelt commenced a campaign in favour of war. Mr. Morton Fullerton denounced Germany which coveted and threatened the two Americas. The President did not change his position. On February 6, 1915, to the great scandal of the Allies in Europe and the pro-Allies in America, he telegraphed birthday greetings to the Emperor

William. Had he then elected—as people dared to write—in favour of the path of cowardice? No indeed, as events soon proved. He was cautiously waiting. He desired peace, not only because he had a horror of war, but also because it was necessary for the success of his reforms and for the maintenance of the unity and liberal ideas of his nation. He passionately wished for peace with an anguish which overcame a will until then quite firm. And he allied himself closely, too closely, with those pacifists who alone were able to help him along a difficult road. He ceased to restrain his natural fire, and spoke as an apostle.

"What a future is before us, my friends! The whole world is troubled. America is alone at peace. Of all the great powers of the world America is the only one to employ its power for the good of the people. America is the only one to use its great character, its great force, in the service of peace and prosperity. Does it not seem probable that one day the world will turn towards America and say, 'You were right, we were wrong. We lost our heads, you kept yours'?"

This is not the language of a statesman, but of an enthusiast. We must never forget, however, that the Presidency of the Republic

of the United States is an office which makes
its occupant partly a popular magistrate, partly
a dictator.   To hold the office well a man must
be both one and the other, an ardent orator, a
cold and resolute administrator.   The tribune
shines on the platform, the dictator in action.
The office is difficult, and, if President Wilson
is himself hard to understand, it is because he
comprehends very well the nature of his
duties.   Sometimes passionate oratory over-
whelms him, as in the present case.   But the
dictator does not sleep.   President Wilson
never fails—as even his opponents recognise
—to take at the necessary moment any essential decisions which will determine the future.

VIII—*Towards War: Deeds*

ONE of these moments now presented itself. At the beginning of 1915 American diplomacy was in an awkward situation. Continuous acts, sometimes on the part of England, sometimes on that of Germany, infringed the regulations of international law. Germany placed all her food supplies under government control. England instantly declared that such food supplies ceased to be a matter of private concern and became of public significance. Ships carrying cargoes of like nature would be conducted for examination and seizure into British ports. This was the first blow directed against international law. But the German counter-attack was graver still. In February, 1915, Berlin announced that England was blockaded, and that consequently the maritime zone encompassing her became a "war zone." If neutrals ventured into this area they must run the risks of their acts. The British decision threatened commercial interests, but the German decree threatened life itself. The double reply of President Wilson marked how clearly he realised the difference. He negotiated with Great Britain. The Note addressed to Berlin was an immediate summons.

"If the commanders of German vessels of war should act on the presumption that the flag of the United States was not being used in good faith and should destroy on the high seas an American vessel or the lives of American citizens, it would be difficult for the Government of the United States to view the act in any other light than as an indefensible violation of neutral rights, which it would be very hard indeed to reconcile with the friendly relations now so happily subsisting between the two Governments.

"If such a deplorable situation should arise, the Imperial German Government can readily appreciate that the Government of the United States would be constrained to hold the Imperial German Government to a strict accountability for such acts of their naval authorities and to take any steps it might be necessary to take to safeguard American lives and property and to secure to American citizens the full enjoyment of their acknowledged rights on the high seas."

Great Britain and Germany replied, and the double negotiation was being conducted with some asperity when German action intervened.

On May 8, 1915, the *Lusitania* was torpedoed
off the southern coast of Ireland. The *Lusitania* was one of those huge liners which carry
the aristocracies of America and Europe with
so much comfort that their easy existence is
scarcely troubled. She was torpedoed without
warning, and amongst the drowned—eleven
hundred in all—one hundred Americans per-
ished.

A cry of horror rose throughout America.
This war she thought so far away, so beyond
her purview, was attacking and wounding her.
Her astonishment was as great as her anger.
New York demanded the rupture of relations
with Germany. The President's decision was
awaited. War! Without question on that
day he could have declared it. On that day,
said many Americans, and from that day on
any day the President was in a position to declare war. The nation would have followed
him. Undoubtedly the shock was violent, and
the incitement keen. But was it as lasting as it
was sharp? Would the nation have followed
him wholly and with unchangeableness, with
the absolute devotion so necessary in the conduct of such a struggle? Listen to the speech
made by Professor Lowell of Harvard. "Let
us imagine that President Wilson had decided
to launch us into war after the torpedoing of

the *Lusitania*. Could the people have stopped
him? No, because everything—amidst the universal waving of flags—would have given place
to excitement. Could President Wilson have
consulted the nation? No, because events
were moving too rapidly. He might have consulted Congress, but Congress is not the nation. And, even had he consulted the nation,
under the circumstances what response would
he have obtained? An emotion—for a nation
passing through such a crisis is able to feel an
emotion but unable to form an opinion. This
emotion was war." * The President had indeed the power, but had he the right?

President Wilson almost certainly remembered that twenty years earlier, in 1898, an
analogous catastrophe had plunged the United
States into another war. The ironclad *Maine*
had been sunk in a Cuban port then belonging
to Spain. Without waiting an instant for reflection or inquiry, the American public held
Spain responsible for the loss of life. President McKinley was swayed by the national
feeling and declared war. In his history of
the American people, President Wilson blames
his predecessor. "The war against Spain was
inevitable and just," he wrote, "but it should

*Speech to the League to impose Peace. *Boston Evening
Transcript,* March 7, 1916.

have been declared after reflection and after preparation." President McKinley allowed himself to be swept off his feet, and, in consequence, the war with Spain was longer, more difficult, and more costly than it should have been. "This war was one of impulse," he wrote again, "and it was clear to see how unprepared we were for a task abruptly undertaken. The United States Army consisted of no more than 28,000 men, officers and soldiers. . . ."

President Wilson did not intend to be swept off his feet. To submit to the contagion of an opinion influenced by passion was repugnant to him, appearing unworthy of his character and of his office. In May, 1915, the United States was in his opinion unprepared materially as well as morally, and he did not wish to urge matters forward.

Three days after the destruction of the *Lusitania* he spoke in public. His speech was an appeal for calmness.

"The example of America must be a special example, and must be an example not merely of peace because it will not fight, but because peace is a healing and elevating influence of the world, and strife is not. *There is such a thing as a man being too proud to fight; there is such a thing as a nation being so right that*

*it does not need to convince others by force
that it is right."*

*There is such a thing as a man being too
proud to fight. . . .* For no words has he been
more often reproached. Friends of the Entente saw in the phrase a want of courage, a
cowardice hidden under the cloak of clever
rhetoric, and, at the same time, a lack of spirit,
a flattery and demagogic wheedling to attract
the pacifists. Meanwhile the President prepared in perfect silence and complete solitude
a Note to Germany. He worked alone upon it,
and called together his Secretaries of State
only to read what had been already written.

On May 13 he issued his reply. Dignified
and firm, the whole of America approved it.
The hand of a statesman was apparent, a man
trained to arrive at the essential point of an
argument, to define it, and to confine himself
to it. President Wilson did not allow that
merchant ships could be torpedoed without
warning and without effort to rescue the
crews. This he repeated, adding that no act
or deed should be omitted by him to uphold the
rights of his fellow citizens. Berlin answered
immediately, but evasively, and raising quite
another question: Was the *Lusitania* armed or
unarmed? The evasion was a smart quibble,
and likely to divide American opinion. Some

of the Secretaries of State weakened. They
telephoned the President and sent him suggested replies. They received no answer.*
Bryan, Secretary of State, resigned. The
President, who had until then been careful
to conciliate him and his followers personally, accepted the resignation. Quitting
Washington, the head of the Senate passed
twenty-five days at Cornish, taking counsel, it
seemed, alone with Colonel House, his intimate
agent, the *eminence grise* of a new Cardinal-
Statesman. The President did not admit the
German subterfuge. On June 10, he repeated
his warning. He insisted upon reparation for
the past and promises for the future. He expressed himself with "a solemn insistence,"
"hoping against hope" that there would be no
need to repeat his protests.

What would be the effect of these words?
In America, as in Europe, the public commenced to smile. To the President's Notes
Berlin always returned a dilatory reply, and,
under the cover of a tricky verbiage, continued
an implacable war. In July, the *Nebraskan,*
an American ship, was torpedoed. In August,
the *Arabic,* belonging to Great Britain, was

*These details have been taken from an energetic article
in the *North American Review,* entitled "The Mystery of
Woodrow Wilson" (September, 1917).

sent down, American lives being lost in the wreck. President Wilson's position became critical. To each German outrage he offered a protest, never allowing the law to lapse through lack of attention. Germany replied by a pretence of promises, sham excuses, suggestions as to enquiry, and always by brutal deeds. In September, 1915, a German submarine torpedoed the Allan liner *Hesperian* one hundred and thirty miles west of Queenstown.

Thus Germany defied America on the high seas. She behaved in the same manner on land, defying America on the very soil of the States. In their own land she endeavoured to stir up the Americans of German birth or origin. And this audacious attempt, of which we knew the existence in Europe although we only partially realised its gravity, rendered President Wilson's position tragic. The German terrorists blew up bridges, burnt factories, and fomented strikes. In August, 1915, whilst the President negotiated, and Berlin counter-balanced his Notes with torpedoing and murder, the *World,* a New York journal, published authentic documents revealing the underground German plots. Even diplomatists were compromised, including a military attaché, a naval attaché, and the Austrian ambassador, Dr. Dumba. The government insti-

tuted proceedings, seized papers, and discovered deeds so grave, so threatening for the United States, that the knowledge of them was kept from the public and silence decided upon.*
At the same moment the Mexican troubles revived, and President Wilson was again confronted with the fantastic activity of those he was henceforward to consider the enemies of his country, of peace itself, and of all human order. Germans were found in the Mexican irregular bands. Their military knowledge gave them authority, and they were often in command. They had received instructions incessantly to endeavour to provoke a conflict between Mexico and the United States. The task was easy. They led their bands to the American holdings, encouraging their followers to pillage, and, if possible, to murder. Many Americans were killed.

Thus, whilst Europe became slowly engulfed in the horror of monotonous slaughter, the war insinuated itself afar, and reached the New World. What was President Wilson able to do? The whole nation had made him the guardian of its honour, and this honour, as it rested in his hands, was being flouted.

*These papers, or at least some of them, were published in September, 1917. They reveal the frightful work of German corruption.

He was roughly told so. He disregarded the outrages, but, better than any one else, he knew how bad the situation was. Should he suddenly commence a more violent policy, declaring war against Germany and Mexico, and in the United States coercing ten or twenty millions of German-Americans, Irish, Jews, and Austrians? Had he the strength? To defend the interests of an immense country, inhabited by one hundred millions of men, he had the disposition of an army of sixty thousand! President Wilson has never uttered a word concerning the anguish and bitterness of his task. However, we can form some idea of it.

There was another aspect. The President was invested with immense, and, to a certain degree, almost illimitable powers. But, on the other hand, these powers were narrowly limited and almost valueless. They were limited to a duration of four years, of which three were almost expired. Would he be re-elected? Yes, perhaps; no, perhaps. To initiate the most formidable action he had before him some twelve or thirteen months of a precarious power, a power already diminished by the approaching close of his term of office. Human institutions, political constructions raised by men, are in themselves essentially weak. All are defective and feeble in some respect or other. Nature has given men the need of government but refused them the instinct of governing. She leaves them groping, trying to supply their deficiencies by artifice. Artifice or heredity. Artifice in the form of an electorate. And whatever may be the advantages of an electorate it can only create a fluctuating power, returning from time to time (four or seven years, it does not matter which period) to interregnums and crises introduced into the constitution by the people themselves. And the stronger and more effectual the created power, so more perilous are these eclipses, so more profound the crises of their refashioning and the more harmful a return of the crises. The Republic of the United States, in other respects so young and brilliant, has its weak spot, its heel of Achilles.

Assuredly President Wilson had in his mind the crisis which would interrupt and possibly terminate his period of office. His adversaries reproached him for it. They accused him, to state the fact in crude terms, of considering his re-election rather than the honour of the United States, and of endeavouring to escape war in order to gain the goodwill of the masses. These imputations can be disregarded. In so solemn a story let only grave thoughts be found. We believe that President Wilson was not able to keep from his calculations the reality of a crisis which would diminish his authority at the moment he had an extreme need for its unimpaired use. Responsible leaders must not be judged too quickly. Trouble must be taken to estimate the task before them. Consider Wilson's problem. He was confronted by the commencement of a civil war. He foresaw an imminent crisis. Germany was against him everywhere, on the sea, in Mexico, even in the United States. He had no army. Noting these aspects of the situation, dare we blame his prudence?

Prudence did not prevent him from taking action. His first wish was for internal peace. Without taking counsel with Congress, he expelled from the United States those diplomatic felons who had been accredited to him. The Austrian Dumba and the two German captains Boy-Ed and Von Papen were put outside the frontier. This action did not turn him aside from the negotiations he had commenced. He desired to obtain German recognition in writing of the right of neutrals to navigate the seas without running peril of death. Painfully, and after much insistence, he obtained what he wanted. Germany would not torpedo mail steamers without warning and necessary precaution. This engagement was dated September 1st. She regretted the torpedoing of the *Arabic,* held herself ready to indemnify the victims, and announced that instructions had been given "so stringent that the recurrence of similar incidents is considered out of the question" (dated October 5th). She promised to spare the merchant vessels in the Mediterranean (dated January 7, 1916). Unquestionably these promises were only Notes answering Notes. But what more did President Wilson want? He was seeking to safeguard a principle, to maintain intact the liberty of his ulterior measures, of his protests and acts. In this he succeeded.

Principles saved and agitators expelled, President Wilson, signifying his will, maintained a straight road amidst grave disorder. In December, 1915, according to custom, he sent his annual message to Congress. He expressed himself in strong terms, and denounced American pro-Germans.

"I am sorry to say that the gravest threats against our national peace and safety have been uttered within our own borders. There are citizens of the United States, I blush to admit, born under other flags, but welcomed under our generous naturalisation laws to the full freedom and opportunity of America, who have poured the poison of disloyalty into the very arteries of our national life; who have sought to bring the authority and good name of our Government into contempt, to destroy our industries wherever they thought it effective for their vindictive purposes to strike at them, and to debase our politics to the uses of foreign intrigue. Their number is not great as compared with the whole number of those sturdy hosts by which our nation has been enriched in recent generations out of virile foreign stocks; but it is great enough to have brought deep disgrace upon us and to have made it necessary that we should promptly make use of processes of law by which we may be purged of their corrupt distempers.

"America never witnessed anything like this before. It never dreamed it possible. . . . Because it was incredible we made no preparation for it. But the ugly and incredible thing has actually come about and we are without adequate Federal laws to deal with it. . . . I urge you to enact such laws. . . . Such creatures of passion, disloyalty, and anarchy must be crushed out."

He asked for further laws. Military training, which in former years had failed to interest him, now aroused his attention. "It would be shameful," he remarked, "if I had learned nothing in fourteen months.

"War is a thing of disciplined might. If our citizens are ever to fight effectively upon a sudden summons, they must know how modern fighting is done, and what to do when the summons comes to render themselves immediately available and immediately effective. And the Government must be their servant in this matter, must supply them with the training they need to take care of themselves and of it. . . . They must be fitted to play the great rôle in the world, and particularly in this hemisphere, for which they are qualified by principle and by chastened ambition to play.

"It is with these ideals in mind that the plans of the Department of War for more adequate national defence were conceived which will be laid before you, and which I urge you to sanction and put into effect as soon as they can be properly scrutinised and discussed."

Such a message but slightly resembles the harangues of the preceding year. President Wilson had recovered his energy for reform and exhibited it at full strength.

In the meanwhile the German terrorists continued their plots. In Pennsylvania they burnt granaries. At Bethlehem and Topeka they blew up munition factories. In Ohio they fo-

mented and provoked strikes and riots. In
New York Harbour a merchant vessel was
scuttled. In Mexico they supplied Huerta and
Villa, and their troops, with money. In the
United States even they organised and armed
Germans who had not been able to mobilise at
their country's call. They prepared a raid
upon Canada. The American police were
aware of the plot and prevented it. But a fire,
the act of an incendiary, completely destroyed
the Canadian parliament buildings. The fever
and fury of the Old World was injuring this
New World, so proud of its youth and honesty. Peace and American unity were being
broken up. President Wilson decided to act,
and, in the popular phrase, to take the bull by
the horns. He announced his intention of con-
ducting an oratorical campaign in favour of
the measures dealing with military training.
He would deliver his first speech in that part of
the States almost wholly peopled by citizens
of German origin.

It was time. Even his own party had commenced to rebel. At the close of January,
1916, the Democrats seemed disposed to delay
the vote upon the military training measures.
Bryan ostentatiously asserted that he was not
joining the tour. The President left Wash-

ington, and the whole country watched a departure of fateful consequence. If the President failed there would be an end of his measures, of his government, of his career. Once more he would become a college professor, and another would occupy his seat.

To follow in the press the various stages of his career gives a curious series of pictures. We are able to perceive the immensity, the want of cohesion, and, at the same time, the greatness of the American people. On the 29th, he was at Pittsburgh, the iron city. The men who worked there were making money, and had other things to do than to listen to speeches. The President was received with indifference, and his meeting was but a partial success. On the 31st, he was at Milwaukee. This city, whose name is unknown in France, is as large as Lyons. The population numbers over 400,000 inhabitants, the majority of foreign extraction. Milwaukee is a German town, and the President stopped there by design. He arrived with a guard, a rare occurrence in the United States. Horse militia escorted his carriage, a line of police separating him from the crowd. In a word, he defied his audience. Then he spoke. At the outset he glorified American patriotism. "America first!" he cried, and, as the public applauded, he tackled the question of the moment.

"In the first place, I know that you are depending upon me to keep this nation out of war. So far I have done that. And I pledge you my word that, God helping me, I will, if it is possible."

A burst of acclamation interrupted his words. He waited, then continued:

"But you have laid another duty on me. You have bidden me see that nothing stains or impairs the honour of the United States. And that is a matter not within my control. That depends on what others do, not upon what the Government of the United States does, and therefore there may be, at any moment, a time when I cannot both preserve the honour and the peace of the United States. Do not exact of me an impossible and contradictory thing, but stand ready and insist that everybody who represents you should stand ready to provide the means for maintaining the honour of the United States."

Again he was cheered, but the acclamation seemed less spontaneous and enthusiastic.

"Do not deceive yourself as to where the colours of your flag came from. Those lines of red are lines of blood, nobly and unselfishly shed by men who loved the liberty of their fellow-men more than they loved their own lives and fortunes. God forbid that we should have to use the blood of America to freshen the colour of that flag, but if it should ever be necessary again to assert the majesty and integrity of those ancient and honourable principles that flag will be coloured once more, and in being coloured will be glorified and purified."

More applause. The proceedings passed off becomingly. The President had dared to come, and that was much.

He left Milwaukee in his campaign train, which stopped from station to station, allowing time for a welcome, a few words, and a popular greeting. Under such circumstances a slightly rough familiarity is to be expected, and does not shock. Mrs. Wilson (the President had recently remarried) accompanied her husband, and the crowd was insistent to see the newly married wife, who was reputed a beauty. A voice cried from the crowd:

"Where is Mrs. Wilson? Stand back, Mr. President, so that we may have a look at her!"

"There she is," replied the President. "She is more pleasant to look at than I am."

"That's true enough."

On the evening of the same day he was at Chicago. The Germans are numerous there, and the police were watchful. On February 2nd he spoke at Kansas City to an audience of 15,000. Kansas City is the centre of a great agricultural district. Its inhabitants, separated from the two oceans by chains of mountains, are entirely engrossed in their cattle breeding and harvests. They ignore world problems. To them there is no difference between a King of Italy and a Prince of Siam. They know only the land, their land. Submarine warfare disturbs them not a jot. Before these men President Wilson delivered one of his most striking addresses. He spoke of the vast world in which they were so little interested. He described ports they had never seen. But their corn, and the meat of their beasts, went to these ports, were loaded in ships and carried to England and France. If these markets were not open, prices could not be so good. The ships therefore required care and protection. This, amongst many others, was one of the duties of the President of the United States. But where would his authority be if he had not behind him an awakened people prepared to lend him their aid?

"You are counting upon me to see to it that the rights of the citizens of the United States, wherever they might be, are respected by

everybody. . . . And I have come out to ask
you what there was behind me in this task.

"You know the lawyers speak of the law
having a sanction back of it. The Judge, as
he sits on his bench, has something back of
him. . . . But when I, as your spokesman and
representative, utter a judgment with regard
to the rights of the United States in its relations to other nations, what is the sanction?
What is the compulsion? . . .

"It is necessary, my fellow citizens, that I
should come and ask you this question. . . .
There may come a time—I pray God it may
never come, but it may, in spite of everything
we do, come upon us, and come of a sudden—
when I shall have to ask: 'I have had my say.
Who stands back of me? Where is the force
by which the majesty and right of the United
States are to be maintained and asserted?'

"I have seen editorials written in more than
one paper of the United States sneering at the
number of notes that were being written from
the State Department to the foreign governments, and asking, 'Why does not the Government act?' And in those same papers I
have seen editorials against the preparation
to do anything whatever effective if these notes
are not regarded. . . . It may be the temper

of some editorial offices, but it is not the temper of the people of the United States.

"I came out upon this errand from Washington. . . . I have been thrilled by the experiences of these few days, and I shall go back to Washington and smile at anybody who tells me that the United States is not wide awake. But, gentlemen, crowds at the stations, multitudes in great audience halls, cheers for the Government, the display—the ardent display as from the heart—of the emblem of our nation, the Stars and Stripes, only express the spirit of the nation; it does not express the organised force of the nation.

". . . The Government asks you to give it arms. The very essentials of the American tradition dictate our demand. The constitution of each state forbids its assembly to restrain the right of carrying arms, a right which belongs to each of us. The founders of our institutions understood from the first that the strength of a nation is to be found in its homes. I do not say the moral strength alone. I say the material strength as well.

"They understood that each man has the right not only to have a vote, but also to have —if he wanted it—a gun. . . . What we are asking from you is this: that the nation may hold arms ready to give to those who, in the case happening, may have to defend it."

When he had spoken the President said to the crowd, "I ask you to let me finish my speech by singing with you 'America.'"

Fifteen thousand men, each waving according to the American custom a little American flag, cheered their leader's suggestion. The President, we are told in the *Sun* of February 3rd, stood in a dramatic attitude, his left hand on his breast, his head thrown back as he sang. When the second verse had died away the crowd wished to sing it again. And Mr. Wilson led their voices with outstretched arms.

He then travelled towards those southern states which formed his native soil. He loved the warm atmosphere of the south. At St. Louis he spoke before 18,000 hearers. Perhaps he was a trifle excited by the events of the tour. The fact remains that his speech was a surprise. No propagandist in favour of the measures for military training, not even Mr. Roosevelt, had expressed himself so strongly. Speaking of the navy, "Do you realise its task?" he asked. "Have you ever considered the enormous extent of our coasts, from Panama to Alaska, from Panama to Maine? No navy in the world has so difficult a task, so heavy a defence. The navy ought, in my judgment, to be incomparably the greatest navy in the world."

What would Great Britain have said, had she not been so occupied elsewhere? The 18,000 auditors roared with enthusiasm. But the press discussed the speech with astonishment. It is time, remarked a Republican organ, for President Wilson to return to the calming influence of Washington.

He returned to find warfare rather than peace. The politicians, and—aggravating addition—some of the foremost of his own party, were in open rebellion. The question was no longer one of secret malevolence, of a tardy vote. Direct action was being initiated, and this included an examination of the whole course of the diplomatic negotiations concerning the submarine war. The essential prerogative of the American presidency was being attacked.

Events had taken a fresh turn since 1916. Great Britain had armed its merchant ships in self-defence, and some of these armed merchantmen had entered and remained in American ports. Germany at once protested, on the ground that these armed ships should be treated in the same manner as warships.

President Wilson refused to admit the contention, but his reply did not close the discussion. The German-Americans declared that Germany had the right to sink without warning ships armed against that nation, and that American citizens who embarked on such ships should be warned of the risk, a risk they undertook alone. Many Americans found these views sensible and just, and were troubled by the silent obstinacy with which President Wilson followed another policy. Unceasingly the German agents worked to develop this uneasiness and bring it to a head. They did not have much difficulty in making friends amongst the six hundred members of Congress.* On February 24, 1916, a kind of panic seized the assembled representatives. A report was spread that the President had spoken during his tour in favour of armed intervention. Suddenly it was realised that war was an inevitable catastrophe. The representatives ap-

*German policy has always endeavoured to please Congress at the expense of the President. A pro-German newspaper wrote on April 21, 1916, "We are the free citizens of a free republic, in which the government, by right and by law, is not our master but our paid servant. . . . We have no sovereign to lead us by right or divine inspiration. We will no longer tolerate a dictator. . . . To assure the unity and solidarity of public action the President must take counsel with Congress before deciding a line of conduct which can lead either to peace or war."

peared willing to act in conjunction with the Committee of Foreign Affairs, and to take a strong hand. A resolution was drafted forbidding Americans to embark upon armed ships.

On that day Germany almost conquered President Wilson, but on that day the singular temper of the man was revealed. Behind him was an uncertain country, before him an aroused Congress. He did not vacillate for an instant. The Chairman of the Committee of Foreign Affairs presented himself, with two important representatives, to acquaint the President of the intention of the two Houses. President Wilson refused to receive them, allowing it to be understood that a letter, then being put together, would give his reply. This letter was addressed to Senator Stone, who had already expressed his uneasiness and his doubts to the President.

"No nation, no group of nations, has the right while war is in progress to alter or disregard the principles which all nations have agreed upon in mitigation of the horrors and sufferings of war, and if the clear rights of American citizens should ever unhappily be abridged or denied by any such action, we should, it seems to me, have in honour no choice as to what our own course should be.

"For my own part, I cannot consent to any abridgement of the rights of American citizens in any respect. . . . To forbid our people to exercise their rights for fear we might be called upon to vindicate them would be a deep humiliation indeed. . . . It would be a deliberate abdication of our hitherto proud position as spokesmen, even amidst the turmoil of war, for the law and the right. . . .

"What we are contending for in this matter is of the very essence of the things that have made America a sovereign nation. She cannot yield them without conceding her own impotency as a nation, and making virtual surrender of her independent position among the nations of the world.

"I am speaking, my dear Senator, in deep solemnity, without heat, with a clear consciousness of the high responsibilities of my office, and as your sincere and devoted friend. If we should unhappily differ, we shall differ as friends, but where issues so momentous as these are involved we must, just because we are friends, speak our minds without reservation."

The American people has a highly developed sense of authority, but a very feeble instinct of parliamentary manners. It applauded the President and hooted the Representatives. A study of the press clearly gives this impression. With the exception of certain pro-German papers, which denounced President Wilson's "secret diplomacy," the press generally approved of their leader's stroke and blamed what it described as "a parliamentary rebellion." The President was appealing to the people, they said. Congress awaited the master's voice. The President had whip in hand.

"Let us recognise," wrote the *Sun,* which was not always favourable to the Administration, "that however badly our affairs may be administered by a single man and his advisors, they would be administered much worse if they were subject to the digressions of 583 senators and representatives. What at the present moment is unsatisfactory would become intolerable in the future. Instead of mistakes we should have chaos. . . . There is not a man of sound sense, who, after Wednesday's exhibition, can imagine for an instant that our foreign affairs would be better conducted if they were under the influences of which we have just witnessed an example. . . . President Wilson's bitterest critic could not wish to substitute in his place a Congress united in plenary sitting."

Public anger was so strong that the representatives abruptly ended their agitation and ran to shelter. President Wilson, considering them humiliated, consented to hear them. On the 25th he received the three emissaries he had shut his door to on the 24th. The interview was curt.

"I intend to see this thing through," said the President.

"The country is of a different opinion," replied the emissaries.

"Events will justify me."

The President's victory lacked one important factor. It had not been sanctioned by a vote. Disturbing rumours were spread. It was said that the President had stated that if the United States entered the war they would shorten the conflict and thus render a great service to civilisation. This assertion was contradicted, but the denials did not end the matter. The President wished to close the discussion. He interviewed an influential representative.

"For some months I have struggled to keep the United States off the edge of a precipice. My task has been immensely increased by members of Congress, who have not been aware of the whole facts of the situation. My hands must be free. This resolution—which I did not desire—has not been the subject of a vote. I wish it to be discussed and rejected."

He was given ample satisfaction. By 64

votes to 14, and by 276 to 142 the Senate and the House of Representatives threw out the resolution forbidding Americans to travel on merchantmen armed against submarines. The Germans had lost their last hope.

On March 24, 1916, the *Sussex,* which crossed the Channel between Folkestone and Dieppe, was torpedoed without warning. The vessel was a mailboat carrying passengers. Amongst the Americans on board were Professor Baldwin, one of President Wilson's colleagues at Princeton, and his daughter, who was seriously injured. The Professor sent the President a personal telegram.

"An American woman travelling within her right, carrying an American passport, struck down on the *Sussex,* and now hovering between life and death, demands reparation for this attempt upon the lives and liberties of Americans."

America was thrilled. Germany had clearly broken the promise given on October 5th, and America found herself in the position of ruptured relations so plainly foreseen and defined by her President. National opinion asserted itself with much energy. Official reports showed that public feeling was shared at the White House. Fifteen days were given to

Germany for an explanation. On April 10
Germany replied that the *Sussex* had been sunk
by an English mine. But the facts were beyond argument. The track of the torpedo had
been seen, and fragments had been recovered.
President Wilson shut himself up, and, for
eight days, worked with his private advisors.
On April 19 he summoned Congress. Without a doubt this step was determined by serious
constitutional considerations. The Constitution of the United States gives the President
the right to conduct negotiations, but reserves
to Congress the right to declare war. It is,
however, often difficult to trace a clear line between the last act of negotiations and the first
act of war. President Wilson found himself
in a position of many alternatives. Without
relinquishing his prerogatives he wished to
make the Congress a responsible witness of the
action he was preparing. "The patience of
the United States is exhausted," he announced.
"Unless the Imperial Government should now
immediately declare and effect an abandonment
of its present methods of warfare against pas-
senger and freight vessels, the Government
can have no choice but to sever diplomatic relations with the Government of the German
Empire altogether." The President spoke

coldly, quietly, and impressively. Senators
and Representatives listened with the gravest
attention. At his last word they rose in mark
of approbation, not as a body but slowly, one
by one, and without enthusiasm.

In Berlin Ambassador Gerard handed a
peremptory note to the German Government,
which, after a few days' silence, replied and
gave way. The Germans would sink merchant
ships only after proper warning and the safety
of the crews. However, the Government took
care not to pledge the future. It demanded
that the British Government should also observe the rules of war with regard to block-
ades. It reserved liberty to act should the Government of the United States of America not
succeed in obtaining from its adversary equal
concessions. President Wilson replied quickly
and concisely. He acknowledged the promise,
adding that he expected its "scrupulous execution." This would avert the *chief* danger
of a rupture of relations, he stated in a curious
phrase. As to the bargain the German Government were endeavouring to strike, he energetically refused to entertain the idea.

"The respect due to American citizens on
the high seas ought not in any manner or
degree to be subject to the conduct of other

governments. . . . The responsibility in this matter is personal, not joint; absolute, not relative."

This was the last word in the dialogue.

IX—*Towards War: Doctrines*

THE President had overcome the Kaiser. The American people celebrated the *"Sussex* pledge" as a national victory. They wanted peace, but they loved prestige. They were happy in having one with the other. The President had always appeared as a man of peace; he remained "the man who kept us out of war." But no one would be able to say that he was the man of a humiliating peace. The nation was thus satisfied with itself and with its head.

The satisfaction was entirely popular. Some one, without doubt, did not share it, and that person was the President himself. Measuring his victory, he was aware of its limits. The German chancellory had given way, but with a formal reserve. It was able at any moment to perjure itself or to withdraw its pledge. The spring of 1915 had produced a tragic surprise—the torpedoing of the *Lusitania.* The spring of 1916 had not been without a similar incident—the torpedoing of the *Sussex.* What surprise had the spring of 1917? And that surprise might come even sooner. Much was possible. Like a clear sky suddenly shrouded in fog, the vast space between Germany and the United States had in an instant become a perilous zone. Submarines on the water, conspiracy on land, diplomatic intrigue in Mexico, all were equally able to cause war. How could it be avoided?

There was no longer time. Silently but actually the war had already attacked the United States, introducing innumerable troubles. The moral unity of the country had been broken, the economic life overthrown. Whilst some were enriched others were being impoverished. Thus were strikes and social crises fomented. Reforms half-planned were interrupted. The situation called for the radical recasting of the military system, and, after the creation of a great fleet the creation of a great army. This European conflagration they had at first considered so far away was gradually drawing nearer. It had surrounded them. They were being held within its fire. "This war," the President had said a few months earlier, "is the last the United States will be able to avoid being dragged into." But the United States was being dragged into it. The American people, still unconscious of their peril, felt deeply that they had the right and the duty to intervene, to arbitrate a peace by every

force a great nation can dispose of, in order
to assure the future against the return of such
a catastrophe.

From that time the idea of intervention occupied the imagination of the American people.
They knew neither the moment nor the manner. But they were sure that history destined
them to act as peacemakers and reformers in
unhappy Europe. Upon this point opinion
agrees. A few, not so numerous as ardent,
cried, "Let us intervene with arms and defend
the right." Others said, "If we intervene we
shall not be able to arbitrate the peace, so do
not let us intervene." But all thought, "peace
will be our doing." Upon that point all were
in complete accord.

In May, 1916, many newspapers, interpret-
ing the public view, reproached the President
for his lack of action. Why did he stop after
his success? Why did he not make use of such
an excellent opportunity? If he proposed himself as arbitrator the belligerents would listen
to him. The President was better informed.
He knew that the belligerents would not listen
to him. He remained silent, reflecting upon the
new task events were preparing for him.

His reflections were mingled with that prudence we have seen from the commencement.
He was pressed to intervene. The conse-

quences of such an act had to be well considered. Intervention would bring the war still closer. At the extreme end of intervention was war, which the President saw always nearer and more threatening. How could his people enter the war united and enthusiastic?

United—that was the first necessity. President Wilson had been watching for two years, and the same policy had to be continued. Between Germans, French, English and Russians he would make no choice. He could show no personal inclination towards any of the foreign causes. He surveilled himself constantly, although there was no question of his own feelings. He was for the Entente and against the Empires. But he forbad himself to show this feeling. If he entered the war it must be for reasons and new principles which would not run counter to the passions of any American.

Enthusiastic—enthusiasm is necessary if democracies are to act. President Wilson knew the American people. He knew that the nation was allied, in spite of its youth, with old Christian and revolutionary movements of Europe. Puritans and persecuted Huguenots were its first ancestors. The ideas and the men of the eighteenth century gave it freedom. The exiles of 1848 (a great number German republicans) asked a refuge of it. The American people has an instinct and desire for noble causes which excite and arouse it. The President knew this. "I would sooner sacrifice," he declared in one of his popular speeches, "a part of our territory than a part of our ideal."

A humanist liberalism is the true religion of the American people. Awaken it to this cry, appeal to it for the defence of such a doctrine, and the nation will give its consent to the sacrifice. An illustrious master, Charles W. Eliot of Harvard, undertook this crusade. Humanity is in danger, he declared. If Prussianism triumphs the liberties of the Anglo-Saxon world are lost. The victorious element will make all conform to its own civilisation, and, setting aside all hoped for reforms, and those already commenced, will militarise their institutions. The Anglo-Saxon world must unite to gain salvation. The United States must enter into alliance with Great Britain and France and fight by their sides. Other public men presented the question in a different form, but their tendency was the same. The Republic of the United States, they said, is based upon peace and can only develop itself in a world of peace. The Prussian state, based upon war, invites humanity to a new order of domination by war. The United States must oppose this order, this Prussian system, by another order,

the system of Peace. Such is the cause, at once
ideal and practical, of the American people. A
league was established to expound it—The
World League to Enforce Peace. It extolled
arbitration and enquiry before conflict. But it
insisted—and in this respect it differed from
the ordinary pacifists—upon the necessity of a
coercive international force, a union of all the
nations of the world, to restrain by force any
nation revolting against the general concert.
Such ideas have taken a strong hold of the
American imagination because they present
many analogies with the constitution of the
United States. The individual states are indeed free, but they are united by a federal
power which determines the diverse interests,
and which represents and guards the common
interests. "The principle of this world organisation [said one of the League's orators]
must be the same as that on which the government of the United States has been based.
When our ancestors founded it the States of
New Jersey and of Virginia abolished their
separate navies. . . . It is the destiny of the
United States to further this idea, for the
United States are themselves the greatest
league for peace that history has acquaintance
with." Perhaps the example given is a special case. It is rash to identify the European

states, as old-fashioned and vehement as religious sects, and these young states which have
grown upon the American prairies. But there
is at least the appearance of an example which
gives life to the theory.*

Mr. Taft, a former President, became president of the League. (We must think of M.
Loubet to establish an analogy.) Some jurists
and university men of importance assisted him.
The League was a success. An American review, the *Outlook,* observed that the single expression of its name wonderfully assisted the
propaganda. The World League to Enforce
Peace. The supporters of unity pronounced
the word "world" with emphasis. The realists
insisted on the word "enforce." The senti-
mentalists strongly accentuated the final word
"peace." The people of the United States felt
at this moment the need to serve an idealistic
cause. Their wealth was prodigious, and it
was good to give, for their gifts in comparison
with their gains were nothing. Reproaches
for this increase of wealth came from all the
European belligerents, from the Allies as well
as from the Central Powers. The people of

*M. Maxime Leroy, in his recent book on *La Société des
Nations* has indicated in detail how American experience has
confirmed and realised the theories enunciated by the League
and President Wilson.

the United States suffered this reproach with impatience. They considered it unjust. They wished to prove to the world that they could renounce as well as profit, could spend as well as gain. They desired also—in the more educated sections of society if not amongst the masses—to prove by their acts that the whole of civilisation had not been dishonoured by the European catastrophe, that one nation at least, and that nation the United States, had not extinguished its hopes, and that Prussia had not gained the day against humanity. The League corresponded sufficiently to the needs of the people, defining a human cause, an American cause, a cause that America as an armed missionary might perhaps have to defend by force. This league satisfied the need of the American people to assert at one and the same time their idealism and their strength.

For May 27, 1916, the League arranged a conference. President Wilson was sounded. Would he appear and speak? He accepted the invitation.

The origins of President Wilson's system of pacifism are not far to seek either in his past career or in his written works. He has been called a late disciple of the eighteenth-century philosophers. This is not exact, for, in politics, his ideas tend to realism and authority. He has also been described as a disciple of Kant. This too is inexact, his ideas are practical, and he is not a moralist. But the United States have on one side been influenced by the eighteenth century, whilst on the other they themselves influenced that dying century and the Revolution. From these facts spring many relationships and the constant possibilities of confusion. A French writer has endeavoured to show that President Wilson has been inspired by Kant.* It would be more true to say that President Wilson inspired Kant, for the principles of American policy which he interprets were known to Kant and his time. Their influence is clear in his "Metaphysik der Sitten" ("Metaphysic of Ethics") and his "Project for Perpetual Peace." †

"In a Congress of many states," wrote Kant, "the question is one of an arbitrary union, dissoluble at any time, and not a union which (like that of the United States of America) would be founded on a public constitution, and therefore indissoluble. In this manner might be formed an institution which would enable men to decide international interests accord-

Revue des Deux-Mondes, February 15, 1917, "Kant et M. Wilson," par César Chabrun.

†"Principes métaphysiques du Droit," trad. Tissot, p. 238.

ing to civil methods, that is to say, like a law suit, and not in the barbarous and savage manner of war."

President Wilson is here the representative of a practice earlier than the theories. Kant deviated from those constitutional principles with which he was dealing. He appeared to foresee an international form of government, in which the various states, raised to a higher moral dignity, would themselves insist upon the respect due to law. President Wilson ignored these dreams. "In his system humanity becomes an organisation with a function to fulfil, an aim to reach," writes M. A. Feïer very ably. "To attain that end humanity has need of a certain proper order, and the elements of this order must be determined according to rule. To ensure the execution of these rules the organism must establish ratifications and assents, to be put into movement by a special power. It is clear then that the contracting system must be replaced by a statutory system; that the autonomous system, solely based upon a categorical command, gives place in Wilson's idea to a heteronomous system which can at need call force to its aid. . . . Still more absurd is the likeness to Rousseau. . . . In contradiction to Rousseau, Mr. Wilson admits a constraint in the name of the law, which limits the liberty of each member and suppresses the possibility of abuse of the rights of one to the detriment of the other members. The Wilsonian system is authority itself, and there is no fear in saying so. In our stage of social evolution and with our present international manners force must be used in the service of right. Pascal wrote that justice and force must be linked together, so that what is just must be also very strong." *

The President adopted the League's ideas with that rapidity and energy which make him so admirable a politician. He saw that these ideas would be very useful to him; useful for his world policy, useful also for his home policy and for the conduct of his Party in which pacifists were so numerous. He also recognised that the proclamation of an ideal would give him a greater moral and semi-religious power. "The force of the majority is the innovation of modern society," he wrote in 1889. "To-day the art of the statesmen is to awaken, to arouse, and to direct this new force." To this art he applied himself, and stood revealed a master. He exerted himself with a calculated lucidity, but also with a poet's ardour.

*"Le Système de M. Wilson," by A. Feïer, *L'Avenir,* August-September, 1917.

He not only inspired and led forward his people. He inspired himself with his people. His sentiments were at once simple and profound, and, in expressing them, he hoped to reach that national unity which was the limit of his efforts.

So, in answer to the League's invitation, he promised to deliver an important speech. His intention was announced some time in advance that public attention might be awakened and his words expected with attention. This speech deserved study. The whole tone was neutral and pacifist, as he intended.

"With the causes and the objects of the Great War we are not concerned," he said. "The obscure foundations from which its stupendous flood has burst forth we are not interested to search for or explore." The effect of the war was to threaten certain of the rights of the United States, and the United States had therefore a word to say in the matter. *"We are not mere disconnected lookers-on."* The President said this for the first time, and the meaning of these plain words, very plainly pronounced, was understood. He continued: "We are participants, whether we would or not, in the life of the world. The interests of all nations are our own also. *We are partners with the rest,* and what affects mankind is in-

evitably our affair as well as the affair of the
nations of Europe and of Asia. . . ." These
were big words for an American statesman,
for, in one stroke, they broke down the separation of the New World from the Old. "We
are a separate people with a separate soul,"
hymned the American people in 1914. In 1916
their President declared that they were a people amongst peoples, members of a common
humanity. He developed his ideas. If we are
participants we have the right to intervene.
Then he added a threat which appears to refer
to Germany.

"It is probable that if it had been foreseen
just what would happen, just what alliances
would be formed, just what forces arrayed
against one another, those who brought the
great contest on would have been glad to substitute conference for force. If we ourselves
had been afforded some opportunity to apprise
the belligerents of the attitude which it would
be our duty to take, of the policies and practices against which we would feel bound to use
all our moral and economic strength, and *in
certain circumstances even our physical
strength,* also our own contribution to the
counsel which might have averted the struggle,
would have been considered worth weighing
and regarding."

President Wilson did not doubt, and has never doubted, that "those who brought the great contest on" are the statesmen of Germany.

He concluded then that the United States should join with other nations in arranging an agreed peace. "This is undoubtedly the thought of America, and what we are going to say at the right moment." He defined the wish of the people of the United States. Firstly, the belligerents should mutually arrange to make peace; secondly, an association of nations should be founded to maintain the freedom of the seas and to prevent any war undertaken in opposition to treaty rights without previous warning and the submission of the litigious claims to the judgment of the world—*a mutual guarantee of territorial integrity and of political independence*. These words are italicized, as they appear to define juridically the understanding the United States will be ready to conclude on the morrow of the war.

The speech of May 27th was considerably discussed. The partisans of the Entente reproached the President for his impenitent neutrality; the conservative Republicans reproached him for his lack of reality, his unmindful ignorance of diplomatic problems.

"A universal association of nations . . ." ironically wrote Mr. Morton Fullerton. "Such, then, is the unstatesmanlike dream of the responsible head of one of the foremost States of the world, almost two years after the outbreak of a war which is being waged in conditions that stultify every possible pretext for harbouring such a dangerous Utopia." *

Would Mr. Morton Fullerton have written those words to-day? The responsible chief of a great democracy speaks always to crowds which are sensible to dreams alone. To attract them he must expound dreams. But he cannot be blamed if at the same time he pursues his own plans. The speech delivered on May 27th is a link in a tight chain. The President's design was to familiarise the people of the United States with the idea of intervention in the European conflict, and he had known well how to do it. The American friends of Germany and the enemies of Great Britain understood and signalled the danger. The *Sun,* for May 29th, protested:

"Do not let us be dragged into foreign alliances. The President proposes nothing less than the reversal of our traditional policy, set-

*"The American Crisis and the War," by William Morton Fullerton, 1916.

ting aside the position which up to the present we have followed so closely."

The *Sun* was right in its statement of the President's attitude, and saw without doubt that although the President spoke insistently of peace it was to lead the people of which he was the head more easily towards war.

X—*Re-election*

FROM this moment the electoral period really commenced. Event rapidly followed event both within and without the United States. For the American people, however, the one factor dominating all others was the expiration of the presidential term of office. Whatever else might be happening this alone pre-occupied their minds.

Would Woodrow Wilson be re-elected? There was no question as to his candidature, which he had announced in February, 1913. In a letter dated February 13, 1913, addressed to Mr. A. Mitchell Palmer he had stated: "Four years is too long a term for a President who is not the true spokesman of the people, who is imposed upon and does not lead. It is too short a term for a President who is doing or attempting a great work of reform and who has not had time to finish it." As adversary he had the republican party, still in possession of its old and powerful prestige, supported by the great financiers, ardent friends of the Entente who bore the President no goodwill for his neutrality, and backed also by the friends of Germany who refused to forgive him for not having forbidden the sale of arms and munitions to the Entente. With him was the mass of the democratic party. It had long been deprived of the advantages of being in power. But, despite petty revolts, it still followed with discipline a leader which honoured and served it. Mr. Wilson was also helped by a tradition which advises the American people to retain a president in office if he merits the privilege. To his credit stood immense work, reforms achieved and in progress, and an unceasing activity which was never absent when called for.

He pressed forward the military training measure. The old regular army consisted of 100,000 men. He wished to increase it to 170,000, with a reserve of 230,000, making 400,000 in all. Behind the first army he planned a second for territorial defence, which would also consist of 400,000 men. Enlistment was to be upon the voluntary principle. But "if the number of volunteers did not suffice to complete the effectives of the battalions, the necessary men would be raised in the militia organisations." The militia included all men between the ages of 18 and 45, and was in fact conscription. President Wilson did not refer to it in his speech, but he wanted and obtained it according to the principles he laid down. On other points, which he considered of lesser importance, he gave way. The War Office wanted the national army to be wholly subordinate to the federal state; the Democrats wished the State Militia kept up under a partial control of the federal military authorities. The President refused to intervene, allowed action to be taken, and his party submitted.

Events soon proved that the concession was not a happy one. Within four months the involved Mexican business became more acute, and the Government of the United States was compelled to seek the aid of arms. Already 5,000 men of the regular army had entered Mexico, under the command of General Pershing, to pursue the irregular bands. A long frontier had to be guarded and President Wilson called out the militia. This immediate test showed sad results. Sixty-three per cent of the men called up had no military training, and many lacked equipment three months after their mobilisation. The press did not spare criticism of the President on this occasion. He remained silent. It may be believed that he was not altogether upset by the clear revelation of his party's blunder.

He had other legislation in hand, notably a measure destined to make the navy second in the world. President Wilson still admitted the maritime supremacy of Great Britain. Another law concerned the mercantile marine. Until then America had been dominated by the old shipping industries of Europe. The President wished to see his country free and owning its own fleet for world commerce as well as for war. He wanted an early creation of what seemed to be a State fleet. Congress did not agree with him, and he gave way. It was settled that the State should not own its own ships more than five years after the conclusion of peace in Europe. However, he had been allowed, on essential consideration, a capital sum of 50,000,000 dollars for purchase and construction. The future was soon to show the urgency of this credit and its great national utility.

This did not complete his plans. President Wilson had not forgotten the domestic legislation he had already initiated. Two measures remained in suspense, one dealing with agricultural credit, the other with child labour in factories. The approaching end of the parliamentary session threatened both. Wishing to save them, the President directly appealed to the party leaders. The measure dealing with child labour presented great judicial difficulties. Promulgated by the central power it applied to the internal affairs of the autonomous states contrary to tradition and the constitution. The President had recognised this several years earlier. "If the federal legislation controlling child labour in factories is passed as proposed," he wrote, "it will furnish a striking example of the extension of the central power, quasi-unlimited and exceeding the written text of the constitution." But President Wilson had a passion for centralised authority, and no religious belief in the written word. He obtained his measure after a sharp conflict with the industrial magnates.*

There remained some domestic legislation,

*This law offers an example of the curious procedure employed by the Federal American State to extend its powers. It does not possess the power to impose legislation upon any particular State with regard to labour. So it acts as follows. It evokes its rights to regulate commercial exchange between the States. It forbids the circulation of products which have not been manufactured according to the standards established by law. This juggling serves its purpose. All industries must conform, unless they renounce the benefits of federal and world markets, and must not employ a child under the age of fourteen. Children under seventeen cannot be employed on night work, or for more than eight hours. An analogous proceeding permits the Government of the United States to establish a censorship after having declared war. The press is allowed every liberty of criticism. But should this become trying postal service is refused. Criticism is not forbidden, but it is smothered.

suddenly improvised, and of a very discussable
nature, which brought the four years of his
first presidency to a close. In August, 1916,
400,000 railway workers—mechanics, guards,
higher-grade engine drivers—imperatively demanded a reduction of their working hours
from nine or ten to eight. The railway corporations refused the demand, and proposed
arbitration. This, in their turn, the men refused, and announced their intention of striking on September 24th. From Philadelphia to
San Francisco, from the great lakes of the
north to New Orleans, all transport would
cease. The threat was a serious one, and the
men had chosen very cleverly the moment to
issue it so roughly. But nine weeks had to
elapse before the date of the presidential election, and the conservative Republicans would
have good cause of quarrel with Mr. Wilson
if a great domestic crisis was the final act of
his administration. The men's leaders called
upon him to deal legislatively with the matter.
He moved with his usual energy, although it
was not an energy displaying much spirit. On
August 29th, he visited Congress in person as
he had done four months earlier to read his
ultimatum to Germany. This time he came
to cede to an ultimatum. He asked for the
immediate voting of a measure which, in its

essentials, would give the railwaymen a legal
day of eight hours. The concession was pain-
ful, and the long presidential speech setting it
forth was found unattractive. President Wilson might have spoken more severely of the
unions which refused arbitration and held their
country by the throat. Amongst the moral
ideas expressed in his message such a judgment would have found a fitting place. But
his words were carefully guarded. He blamed
the companies rather than the syndicates. He
might have recalled the fact that he was not
unequipped should the country need protection
against the blackmail of a corporation. He
allowed the opportunity to pass, and his urgent
need of the favour of the masses—and their
vote—appeared a trifle too clearly. On August
31st the measure was voted with few modifications. The strike did not take place. This
was the last and the least glorious of his victories.

Six years earlier this man had been a university professor of distinction. Since then his
work had been enormous. The people of the
United States were conscious of the control of
a leader, and such control is to their taste.
They do not resist personal power, but rather
greet it with acclamation. Some of their "in-

tellectuals" endeavour to fight against this national impulse, but without effect. Mr. George
E. Boren denounced in the *Sun* the "Darwinian policy," introduced into the United States
both in doctrine and in deed by the Professor-
President Wilson. "Constitutions are what
politicians make them," he wrote. "As President, what did he do with the Government of
the United States? He humiliated it. He
made it submit to the threat of a strike. He
seriously attacked the freedom of the States.
He threatened the freedom of industry in making the central power the purchaser and the
exploiter of a fleet. The Constitution, thus
understood, signifies no more than what can
be demanded by public opinion—at any moment a prey to heresy or hysterics." Mr.
George E. Boren spoke unjustly. The Constitution, as understood by President Wilson,
does not obey the caprice of public opinion. It
essentially obeys a leader who knows public
opinion, who interprets it with freedom and
gives it his direction. Such is his doctrine and
such his practice. He has to submit, to yield,
to bend low in his concessions. He has to act
the part of a demagogue, a necessity under a
democratic régime. But he is a dictator and
not a demagogue.

Listen to his dictatorial voice. On Septem-

ber 2, 1916, he delivered his first speech of
the electoral campaign. He recalled his economic and social work, the revision of tariffs,
the creation of a merchant marine, of a federal
bank, of a national service for labour registra-
tion, of federal regulation for the protection
of child labour. He enumerated with simplic-
ity a succession of victories. The enumeration
alone sufficed his pride. He then turned to
foreign problems. With feeble Mexico he had
been patient. He congratulated himself upon
a policy he intended to continue. He had protested strongly against methods of war on
the seas which had destroyed so many American lives. He congratulated himself on this
policy also, which would be continued. He
would fight to his last breath against those
American citizens who, traitors to America,
remained loyal to their former nationality.
Then for the future. President Wilson discussed the new problems, immense and limitless
prospectives opened up by the Great War. He
did not utter a word which enabled any one to
guess the future action of the United States
in that war. His policy forbad him. But he
asserted with force that the United States
would participate in the peace. What did he
mean? To participate in peace one must first
participate in war. These were his words:

"There must be a just and settled peace, and we here in America must contribute the full force of our enthusiasm and of our authority as a nation to the organisation of that peace upon world-wide foundations that cannot easily be shaken. No nation should be forced to take sides in any quarrel in which its own honour and integrity and the fortunes of its own people are not involved; but no nation can any longer remain neutral as against any wilful disturbance of the peace of the world. The effects of war can no longer be confined to the areas of battle. No nation stands wholly apart in interest when the life and interests of all nations are thrown into confusion and peril. If hopeful and generous enterprise is to be renewed, if the healing and helpful arts of life are indeed to be revived when peace comes again, a new atmosphere of justice and friendship must be generated by means the world has never tried before. The nations of the world must unite in joint guarantees that whatever is done to disturb the whole world's life must first be tested in the court of the whole world's opinion before it is attempted.

"These are the new foundations the world must build for itself, and we must play our part in the reconstruction, generously and without too much thought of our separate interests. We must make ourselves ready to play it intelligently, vigorously, and well. . . . We can no longer indulge our traditional provincialism. We are to play a leading part in the world drama whether we wish it or not. We shall lend, not borrow; act for ourselves, not imitate or follow; organise and initiate, not peep about, merely to see where we may get in.

"This world peace must bring its reward. The fruits of the earth must be raised and exchanged. The United States will do its share, a great share, in this work of human renaissance. Nations will have urgent needs which must be satisfied. American exporters will be given assistance. If any portion of the laws directed against trusts hinder the combination of these traders the laws will be revised. Their foreign enterprises will not be hindered.

"The field will be free, the instrumentalities at hand. . . . The Government of the United States will insist upon the maintenance throughout the world of conditions of fairness and of evenhanded justice in the commercial dealings of the nations." The President finished his speech with a moving peroration:

"The day of Little Americanism with its narrow horizons . . . its methods of 'protection,' is past and gone. . . . A day of enterprise has at last dawned for the United States, whose field is the wide world. . . . We hope to see the stimulus of that new day draw all America, the republics of both continents, on to a new life and energy and initiative in the great affairs of peace. We are Americans for Big America, and rejoice to look forward to the days in which America shall strive to stir the world without irritating it or drawing it on to new antagonisms. . . . Upon this record and in the faith of this purpose we go to the country."

Election day drew near. Who would be successful? Would Wilson gain the day? Nothing was certain. Wilson's personal position was strong, but his electoral difficulties were numerous. In 1912 he succeeded, owing to the division of his opponents' party. Had the votes obtained by the Progressist Roosevelt and the Republican Taft been massed against him he would have been in a minority of 1,300,000. But now the Progressives and Republicans had united. Hughes, a former Governor of the State of New York, one of the nine judges of the Supreme Court, a capable man but without magnetism, was their candidate. Wilson had first to turn over 1,300,000 votes. It was a large number, and even the most confident had their doubts. The war no longer pre-occupied the electorate which was solely interested in the speeches and personalities of Wilson and Hughes. Every one was excited by the race between the two men.

A glance must be taken of the President at home. Miss Ida M. Tarbell, a journalist of much ability, has given us the opportunity. We see him in his country house at Shadow Lawn. He meets his visitor with a hearty welcome; he is amiable because he has decided to be amiable. "A President certainly, always the President, but also a gentleman who, having invited you to his table, treats you as a friend, interests himself in the things you are interested in, and has the frank goodwill not to speak to you but to gossip with you." He touches upon political questions if the visitor asks him, but his comment is one of detachment. He is President, he governs according to his conscience. If he is re-elected he will do his best. If he is not re-elected he will return to his university life. He stands ready to serve, and he awaits the call. Miss Tarbell asks him what he reads.

"For fourteen years I have not read a serious book," he answers. "Detective stories are the only ones which hold me. There are too many problems in modern novels. I have enough problems. Sometimes I read a little verse, and re-open one of my favourite poets. There are passages in Tennyson which have been of great help to me. I do not know of any one who has expounded better than Tennyson the theory of popular government. Do you remember these lines?

> A nation yet, the rulers and the ruled,
> Some sense of duty, something of a faith,
> Some reverence for the laws ourselves have made,
> Some patient force to change them when we will,
> Some civic manhood firm against the crowd.

"Firm against the crowd!" repeated the President. *"Firm against the crowd,* that is the difficulty, the danger."

He recalled to his interviewer the resistance he had been obliged to put up against certain fanatical excitements. But the recollections were neither bitter nor sad. The President had no doubt of the solidarity of agreement which united him to his people.

"I do not think there is a man living more soaked in American thought than I am. I have lived with it all my life. When I try to disentangle the ideas of the people and endeavour to express them if at first there is disaccord I am not astonished. I have firm confidence that their ideas will rally to mine. I much prefer a decision based upon reflection to one founded in haste."

We will follow the subject of our study to one of those meetings where thousands of auditors listened with astonishing silence and self-control to the presidential candidates. On October 26, 1916, Wilson spoke at Cincinnati. He attacked the banking interests, whose monopoly had been overthrown by the Federal Bank he had instituted.

"Have we freed ourselves," he demanded, "in order that newcomers should impertinently become our masters? I will not undertake to direct your affairs, and you know——"

"You do it very well," cried the crowd with cheers.

"No, dear citizens," he answered, "I am only trying to understand what you wish me to do, and that I do."

How suddenly this professor has left the heights! A moment ago he was reciting Tennyson to us. We were shadowed by an Oxford. Now we have been abruptly transported to a Cincinnati, an Ohio.

Another day he spoke at Omaha in Nebraska. The vanished Indians have left behind nothing but the sounds of their musical language. Nebraska is one of the central

states, the Atlantic and the Pacific being at
equal distance. It is almost wholly an agricultural state, the population being indifferent
to everything outside the borders of its own
territory. President Wilson was welcomed at
Omaha. He had maintained peace. That was
all they knew, but it was enough to make them
love and cherish him. He received a great reception, which had all the signs of a pacifist
manifestation.

"He has kept us out of war!" cried somebody
in the crowd.

It was an agreeable cry, which others repeated.

"Who has saved the country?" shouted another.

"Wilson!" replied the crowd with one voice.

"Hurrah for the peacemaker."

President Wilson knew that it was to his advantage that the mob should credit him with
the preservation of peace. But he knew that
it would be hardly possible to maintain peace
longer. His position was delicate. To exploit
this credit would be a powerful but dishonest
method towards immediate success. He behaved, on the contrary, like an honest man,
considering that in such a case honesty was the
best line his policy could pursue. He warned
the over-happy crowds on every occasion. He

had indeed maintained peace. He accepted
their thanks, for he maintained it with much
trouble. But this trouble was in itself a sign
of peril, and the people of the United States
must hold themselves ready against the continuous menace of war, a menace which stead-
ily became more threatening. More than once
he spoke to this effect.

The reception at Omaha disquieted him,
and he replied to the pacifist manifestation with
the most ardent and the most energetic speech
he had delivered. It was a speech of warning.
At first he recalled to the people of Nebraska
the rude history of their early origins, the land
conquered from the Indians, occupied and
cleared by armed cultivators. Then, with a
swift transition, he introduced the subject of
the war.

"There is as much combativeness in America as in any other nation of the world.

"We have a programme for our domestic
life in America, and we will not forget it. But
we have never formulated with the desired
clearness our programme for things outside
America, for the part she must play in the
world. We must imperatively see to this without delay.

"We have never forgotten, as you know,
and we have always treated his words with

respect, the advice of our great Washington. He told us to keep free of compromising foreign affairs. He meant by that, if I understand him well, that we must not become entangled in the ambitions and secret schemes of other nations. But he did not wish to say —and here I must be permitted to risk an interpretation of the words of this great man— that we ought to evade the mutual agreements of the world. For we are part of the world, and cannot be indifferent towards anything that takes place in it.

"The whole world knows this. We are ready to draw upon our forces without reserve to preserve peace in the interests of humanity. What troubles the whole world concerns the whole world. Our duty is to place all our strength at the service of a League of Nations instituted to repress any one endeavouring to disturb peace.

"If any one asks you, 'Are you ready to fight?' answer, 'Yes, I am ready to fight for a cause worth fighting for.' You are not going to fight over any paltry trouble. You are only interested in a single quarrel—that which concerns the Rights of Man. Human blood must be spilt, if necessary, but it must be spilt for a noble cause. The title deeds of liberty are sealed with the blood of free men."

The President spoke with warmth, and the people of Nebraska cheered him, according to the *New York Tribune,* at each sentence. Did these distant inhabitants understand him? It is not certain. But could the President, without creating panic, have said more? He was not able.

He warned the pacifists. More categorically he cautioned the German-Americans. The president of a league which favoured their ideas sent him a telegram.

"Again we greet you with popular disapproval of your pro-British policies. Your failure to secure compliance with all American rights, your leniency towards the British Empire, your approval of war loans and ammunition traffic, are the issues of this campaign."

The answer was immediate. And with it was published the provocatory telegram.

"Your telegram received. Would feel deeply mortified to have you, or anybody like you, voting for me. Since you have access to many disloyal Americans, and I have not, I will ask you to convey this message to them.

WOODROW WILSON.

On the morning of November 7th the result was in doubt. That was not surprising in so disputable and difficult an election. What was surprising, what in fact was laughable (if the

phrase be permitted concerning so serious a
matter), were the shabby tricks and the un-
seasonableness of the difficulties. In November, 1916, there was but one question for the
United States to decide. That question was
the Great War. Would they be actors or spec-
tators? This was the thought in the chancel·
lories of Europe and at the White House. But
for the people of the United States the problem was too complex. The information at
hand was too immense and yet too vague. The
people, not knowing, said nothing. The two
candidates did not ask for a mandate, and no·
body attempted to dictate one. The only question which mattered was not asked. Nothing
else was substituted. In America as in Europe the catastrophe had suspended activity.
Thus the double campaigns of Wilson and
Hughes were characterised by an entire ab-
sence of programmes. Both men exhibited
themselves to the electors and spoke. But they
proposed no reform and no decision. They
were empty handed. And in such a vacuum
how could the chances be measured, or the result foretold? How were the German-Americans going to cast their votes? Vain question.
The German-Americans, equally affronted by
both candidates, would vote according to
chance local intrigue. The feminine vote

would participate for the first time in a presidential election to the tune of three or four millions. To whom would the women give preference? Vain question. The votes of the women will follow those of the men in this dull contest. The result alone could give the answer.

It had to be waited for. The scrutiny was as slow to unravel as it was difficult to anticipate. The first returns were deceptive. The two great eastern states, Pennsylvania and New York, voted as a whole against Wilson. They elected 82 delegates. Illinois followed them with 29. Wilson was thus handicapped from the start by 111 votes. The Republican press in New York lit the beacon fires of victory and announced in giant headlines:

Hughes elected with 290 votes.
Possibly 312. 7 doubtful States.

The news reached Europe, and for twenty-four hours Wilson was believed to have been defeated. He was then able to count his real friends, and the list was not a long one. But, during the afternoon of November 8th, there was a new atmosphere of doubt. Feeble but numerous majorities in the Western and Southern States reversed the prognostics. By the evening of the 10th Wilson had received

251 votes, Hughes 242. The total number of votes being 531, at least 266 were necessary for election. Wilson still had a chance. By the evening of the 11th he held it, although always doubtfully. The results from California and Minnesota remained to be collected, but as the returns were disputed the counting could not be completed. California had 900,000 electors. A democratic majority of 3,700 was worth 13 delegates to Wilson. Minnesota had 360,000 electors. A majority of 500 votes would give Wilson 12 delegates.

The election finished. Wilson received 276 electoral votes; Hughes 255. Counted in popular votes, the figures were as follows:

> Wilson (Democratic) 9,116,296
> Hughes (Republican) 8,547,474
> Benson (Socialist)............... 750,000
> Various 235,206

President Wilson had thus obtained 2,800,-000 votes more than at his first election. This gain was not entirely owing to a turn-over of votes. New electors were numerous, the voting body having been increased by three and one-half millions in four years.

The figures were much discussed in order to arrive at the significance of the votes. There was nothing to find. Infinitely small causes appeared to have determined a majority in one place and another.

If any feeling had influenced the issue it was without doubt the moderation and prudence of the masses. They knew Wilson. He had governed without calamity in a period of calamity. He had tolerably well kept his word. They would keep him. *"Let us keep this proven man!"* had been one of the most convincing cries of the election.

The "chosen man" had now before him four years of supreme magistrature—and the last four. Thus liberated from electoral preoccupations he was free to devote himself exclusively to the good of his country, and, as the old writers used to say, to its proper glory. How strangely history forms itself. This absolute rule which limits the presidential power to two terms of office had its origin in the voluntary resignation of Jefferson. The old democrat wished to prevent by the example he gave any ulterior return to personal power. Assuredly he did not foresee that such limitation would one day have for its effect the increase of presidential power, would render it for a short but sufficient period even dictatorial.

WE now reach the end. The events we are relating extend to the present day. They belong more to the present than to the past, and the time has not yet come when it will be possible to deal with them as a whole.

What will the new President do? Will he intervene? A strong trend of opinion desired it, and wished him to propose mediation. The President had his own serious reasons for listening to this popular demand. He could not ignore that the Germans were constructing new submarines, and preparing for a resumption of their submarine war. The third spring would bring a fresh crisis. This would be the third, and the President believed it would be decisive, making war inevitable. But he did not wish war to surprise him. It was coming, and he saw it coming. So he prepared to meet the cataclysm adroitly. His first step was an appeal for peace, a demand to the belligerents to reveal their intentions and aims. The President considered the terms of this appeal, and, despite his usual habit of secrecy, the news spread. On November 23rd his project was known at Berne, Vienna, and Berlin. Active discussion ensued. Washington issued an official denial which scarcely calmed the rumour. On November 26th Ambassador Gerard was at Washington. He saw the President, dined with Ambassador Bernstorff and immediately returned to Berlin. There, speaking at a banquet, he allowed it to be understood in guarded words that a resumption of submarine warfare would interrupt the good relations existing between Germany and the United States. December had been reached. The President was continuously at work. Undoubtedly his plan was to publish a pacific appeal at the moment of the Christmas festival. But another rumour—springing from Vienna or Berlin—had been placed in circulation. A mysterious event was to take place. The Reichstag was summoned for December 12th, and a speech from the Chancellor was promised. On the day announced he spoke, and launched an appeal for peace.

Was it by chance? Hardly. This idea had been ripening for a long while in America, and Bethmann-Hollweg seized hold of it at the very moment another statesman was about to make it his own. The tactics were clever. The German Chancellory did not wish another to

have the benefit of so fine an attitude. Well
acquainted with the deeds in preparation for
the following April it made a wily move to
excuse the brutalities which would ensue. The
appeal was addressed to neutral states. "We
are persuaded that the propositions we offer,
which aim at the certainty of the future existence, honour, and development of our nation,
may well serve as the foundation of a durable
peace. If, in spite of this offer of peace and
conciliation, the fight must continue, the four
Allied Powers are determined to pursue it to a
victorious conclusion, solemnly, before humanity and before history, declining all responsibility."

President Wilson had been decidedly
thwarted. Once again Prussia had been the
first to mobilise, and, by her quickness of movement, had disconcerted her adversary. What
was he to do? Could he renounce the whole
project because he had lost the first move? He
persisted with his plan, and on December 18th
published the appeal he had had in preparation.

This appeal was extremely prudent. President Wilson declined "to propose peace, even
to offer mediation." He suggested only "that
some soundings might be taken, so that it could
be discovered how far we are from that haven
of peace towards which all humanity yearns

with an intense and gathering force." He indicated certain points upon which the belligerents appeared to be in agreement, and also the necessity of a liberal, durable, and guaranteed peace. He also announced, and these words were the most significant in his appeal, that if the war continued "the situation of neutral nations, already very difficult, would become wholly impossible."

At first sight the coincidence of the two notes was astonishing. Germany had appealed to the neutrals. The most powerful of the neutral states appeared to have replied to her appeal. Some people even thought that President Wilson, in agreement with Germany, was busying himself to impose the peace she was asking for. There was certainly some appearance of it.

The Entente answered with courtesy, and in detail. The Central Empires replied in ten lines with transparent disdain. Was this the end? Could there be no other result to documents which had provoked such mixed feelings of anger, hope, and expectation? The President pursued his way. On January 21, 1917, he appeared in the Senate and read a long message which astonished profoundly both chancelleries and nations. Setting aside the contingencies of war and peace, the President outlined the existence of a Society of Nations, which, he asserted, the people of the United States had as a mission to establish. It was not the first time he had dealt with the subject, which he had referred to in a speech upon a League to enforce Peace made before Congress on May 27, 1916. He now developed these principles, and the text of his message must be given in full.

PRESIDENT WILSON'S MESSAGE TO THE
AMERICAN CONGRESS

COMMUNICATED TO THE BELLIGERENT STATES

(*Known as the Note of January 22, 1917*)

Gentlemen of the Senate,

On the 18th of December last I addressed an identic Note to the Governments of the nations now at war requesting them to state, more definitely than they had yet been by either group of belligerents, the terms upon which they would deem it possible to make peace.

I spoke on behalf of humanity and of the rights of all neutral nations like our own, many of whose most vital interests the war puts in constant jeopardy.

The Central Powers united in a reply which stated merely that they were ready to meet their antagonists in conference to discuss terms of peace.

The Entente Powers have replied much more definitely, and have stated, in general terms indeed, but with sufficient definiteness to imply details, the arrangements, guarantees, and acts of reparation which they deem to be the indispensable conditions of a satisfactory settlement.

We are much nearer a definite discussion of the peace which shall end the present war. We are that much nearer the discussion of the international concert which must thereafter hold the world at peace. In every discussion of the peace that must end this war it is taken for granted that peace must be followed by a definite concert of the Powers which will make it virtually impossible that any such catastrophe should ever overwhelm us again. Every lover of mankind, every sane and thoughtful man, must take that for granted.

I have sought this opportunity to address you because I thought that I owed it to you, as the council associated with me in the final determination of our international obligations, to disclose to you without reserve the thought and purpose that have been taking form in my mind with regard to the duty of our Government in the days to come, when it will be necessary to lay afresh and upon a new plan the foundations of peace among the nations.

It is inconceivable that the people of the United States should play no part in that great enterprise. To take part in such a service will be the opportunity for which they have sought to prepare themselves by the very principles and purposes of their polity and the approved practices of their Government ever since the days when they set up a new nation in the high and honourable hope that it might in all that it was and did show mankind the way to liberty. They cannot in honour withhold the service to which they are now about to be challenged. They do not wish to withhold it. But they owe it to themselves and to the other nations of the world to state the conditions under which they will feel free to render it.

That service is nothing less than this: To add their authority and their power to the authority and force of other nations to guarantee peace and justice throughout the world. Such a settlement cannot now be long postponed. It is right that before it comes this Government should frankly formulate the conditions upon which it would feel justified in asking our people to approve its formal and solemn adherence to a league for peace. I am here to attempt to state those conditions.

The present war must first be ended, but we owe it to candour and to a just regard for the opinion of mankind to say that, so far as our participation in guarantees of future peace is concerned, it makes a great deal of difference in what way and upon what terms it is ended.

The treaties and agreements which bring it to an end must embody terms that will create a peace that is worth guaranteeing and preserving, a peace that will win the approval of mankind, not merely a peace that will serve the several interests and immediate aims of the nations engaged.

We shall have no voice in determining what those terms shall be, but we shall, I feel sure, have a voice in determining whether they shall be made lasting or not by the guarantees of a universal covenant; and our judgment upon what is fundamental and essential as a condition precedent to permanency should be spoken now, not afterwards, when it may be too late.

No covenant of co-operative peace that does not include the peoples of the New World can suffice to keep the future safe against war; and yet there is only one sort of peace that the peoples of America could join in guaranteeing. The elements of that peace must be elements that engage the confidence and satisfy the principles of the American Government, elements consistent with the political faith and the practical convictions which the peoples of America have once for all embraced and undertaken to defend.

I do not mean to say that any American Government would throw any obstacle in the way of any terms of peace the Governments now at war might agree upon, or seek to upset them when made, whatever they might be. I only take it for granted that mere terms of peace between the belligerents will not satisfy even the belligerents themselves. Mere agreements may not make peace secure.

It will be absolutely necessary that a force be created as a guarantor of the permanency of the settlement so much greater than the force of any nation now engaged or any alliance hitherto formed or projected, that no nation, no probable combination of nations, could face or withstand it. If the peace presently to be made is to endure, it must be a peace made secure by the organised major force of mankind.

The terms of the immediate peace agreed upon will determine whether it is a peace for which such a guarantee can be secured. The question upon which the whole future peace and policy of the world depends is this: Is the present a struggle for a just and secure peace

or only for a new balance of power? If it be
only a struggle for a new balance of power,
who will guarantee, who can guarantee, the
stable equilibrium of the new arrangement?
Only a tranquil Europe can be a stable Europe.
There must be, not a balance of power, but a
community of power; not organised rivalries,
but an organised common peace.

Fortunately, we have received very explicit
assurances on this point.

The statesmen of both of the groups of nations now arrayed against one another have
said, in terms that could not be misinterpreted,
that it was no part of the purpose they had in
mind to crush their antagonists. But the im-
plications of these assurances may not be
equally clear to all—may not be the same on
both sides of the water. I think it will be serviceable if I attempt to set forth what we understand them to be.

They imply, first of all, that it must be a
peace without victory.

I beg that I may be permitted to put my own
interpretation upon it, and that it may be understood that no other interpretation was in
my thought. I am seeking only to face realities, and to face them without soft conceal-
ments.

Victory would mean peace forced upon the

loser, a victor's terms imposed upon the van-
quished. It would be accepted in humiliation,
under duress, at intolerable sacrifice, and would
leave a sting, a resentment, a bitter memory
upon which terms of peace would rest, not per-
manently, but only as upon quicksand. Only a
peace between equals can last—only a peace
the very principle of which is equality and a
common participation in a common benefit.
The right state of mind, the right feeling between nations, is as necessary for a lasting
peace as is the just settlement of vexed questions of territory or of racial and national
allegiance.

The equality of nations upon which peace
must be founded, if it is to last, must be an
equality of rights; the guarantees exchanged
must neither recognise nor imply a difference
between big nations and small, between those
that are powerful and those that are weak.
Right must be based upon the common
strength, not upon the individual strength, of
the nations upon whose concert peace will
depend.

Equality of territory or of resources there,
of course, cannot be, nor any sort of equality
not gained in the ordinary peaceful and legitimate development of the peoples themselves.
But no one asks or expects anything more than

an equality of rights. Mankind is looking now for freedom of life, not for equipoises of power.

And there is a deeper thing involved than even equality of right among organised nations.

No peace can last, or ought to last, which does not recognise and accept the principle that Governments derive all their just powers from the consent of the governed, and that no right anywhere exists to hand peoples about from potentate to potentate as if they were property.

I take it for granted, for instance, if I may venture upon a single example, that statesmen everywhere are agreed that there should be a united, independent, and autonomous Poland, and that henceforth inviolable security of life, of worship, and of industrial and social development should be guaranteed to all peoples who have lived hitherto under the power of Governments devoted to a faith and purpose hostile to their own.

I speak of this, not because of any desire to exalt an abstract political principle which has always been held very dear by those who have sought to build up liberty in America, but for the same reason that I have spoken of the other conditions of peace which seem to me clearly

indispensable—because I wish frankly to un-
cover realities.

Any peace which does not recognise and accept this principle will inevitably be upset. It
will not rest upon the affections or the convictions of mankind. The ferment of spirit of
whole populations will fight subtly and constantly against it, and all the world will sym-
pathise. The world can be at peace only if its
life is stable, and there can be no stability
where the will is in rebellion, where there is
not tranquillity of spirit and a sense of justice,
of freedom, and of right.

So far as practicable, moreover, every great
people now struggling towards a full development of its resources and of its powers should
be assured a direct outlet to the great highways
of the seas.

Where this cannot be done by the cession of
territory, it no doubt can be done by the neu-
tralisation of direct rights of way under the
general guarantee which will assure the peace
itself. With a right comity of arrangement no
nation need be shut away from free access to
the open paths of the world's commerce.

And the paths of the sea must alike in law
and in fact be free. The freedom of the seas
is the *sine qua non* of peace, equality, and co-
operation.

No doubt a somewhat radical reconsideration of many of the rules of international practice hitherto thought to be established may be necessary in order to make the seas indeed free and common in practically all circumstances for the use of mankind; but the motive for such changes is convincing and impelling. There can be no trust or intimacy between the peoples of the world without them. The free, constant, unthreatened intercourse of nations is an essential part of the process of peace and of development. It need not be difficult either to define or to secure the freedom of the seas if the Governments of the world sincerely desire to come to an agreement concerning it.

It is a problem closely connected with the limitation of naval armaments and the co-operation of the navies of the world in keeping the seas at once free and safe, and the question of limiting naval armaments opens the wider, and perhaps more difficult, question of the limitation of armies and of all programmes of military preparation. Difficult and delicate as these questions are, they must be faced with the utmost candour and decided in a spirit of real accommodation, if peace is to come with healing in its wings, and come to stay. Peace cannot be had without concession and sacrifice.

There can be no sense of safety and equality

among the nations if great and preponderating armaments are henceforth to continue here and there to be built up and maintained. The statesmen of the world must plan for peace and nations must adjust and accommodate their policy to it as they have planned for war and made ready for pitiless contest and rivalry.

The question of armaments, whether on land or on sea, is the most immediately and intensely practical question connected with the future fortunes of nations and of mankind.

I have spoken upon these great matters without reserve and with the utmost explicitness, because it has seemed to me to be necessary if the world's yearning for peace was anywhere to find free voice and utterance.

Perhaps I am the only person in high authority amongst all the peoples of the world who is at liberty to speak and hold nothing back. I am speaking as an individual, and yet I am speaking also, of course, as the responsible head of a great Government, and I feel confident that I have said what the people of the United States would wish me to say.

May I not add that I hope and believe that I am in effect speaking for liberals and friends of humanity in every nation and of every programme of liberty? I would fain believe that I am speaking for the silent mass of mankind everywhere who have yet had no place or opportunity to speak their real hearts out concerning the death and ruin they see to have come already upon the persons and the homes they hold most dear.

And in holding out the expectation that the people and Government of the United States will join the other civilised nations of the world in guaranteeing the permanence of peace upon such terms as I have named I speak with the greater boldness and confidence because it is clear to every man who can think that there is in this promise no breach in either our traditions or our policy as a nation, but a fulfilment, rather, of all that we have professed or striven for.

I am proposing, as it were, that the nations should with one accord adopt the doctrine of President Monroe as the doctrine of the world: that no nation should seek to extend its polity over any other nation or people, but that every people should be left free to determine its own polity, its own way of development, unhindered, unthreatened, unafraid, the little along with the great and powerful.

I am proposing that all nations henceforth avoid entangling alliances which would draw them into competitions of power, catch them in a net of intrigue and selfish rivalry, and disturb their own affairs with influences intruded from without. There is no entangling alliance in a concert of power. When all unite to act in the same sense and with the same purpose all act in common interest and are free to live their own lives under a common protection.

I am proposing government by the consent of the governed; that freedom of the seas which in international conference after conference representatives of the people of the United States have urged with the eloquence of those who are the convinced disciples of liberty; and that moderation of armaments which makes of armies and navies a power for order merely, not an instrument of aggression or of selfish violence.

These are American principles, American policies. We could stand for no others. And yet they are the principles and policies of forward-looking men and women everywhere, of every modern nation, of every enlightened community. They are the principles of mankind and must prevail.

WOODROW WILSON.

"These are American principles, American policies." The President had fitly spoken, for the country applauded his message. The nation recognised his profound ideals, thus defined and proclaimed in the face of a world dishonoured by massacre. And, in making this answer, he was unable to measure the immensity and the nearness of the sacrifices these ideas were about to drag from him.

The next step followed rapidly. Perhaps President Wilson had imagined that his solemn declarations might be a warning to Germany, obliging her to postpone the resumption of submarine war. He was deceived. His message was delivered on January 21st. On the 31st, in the evening, the German ambassador presented a note which is one of the most extraordinary diplomatic documents of our time. At first unctuous and insipid, then brutal, it is a clever concoction of old Germany and Prussia. The German Government had studied the President's message. "It is pleasing to state that the main lines of this important manifestation are in accord with the principles and desires to which Germany subscribes." And the author of the note complaisantly cited the right of every nation to decide its own destiny and to receive equal treatment, the opposition to any system of alliances, the liberty of the seas, and the policy of an open door to the commerce of all countries. He promised "the joyful collaboration of the German Government in every effort which tended towards the prevention of future wars. Had the Government not once already proposed peace! And suddenly, the verbiage having been long enough drawn out, the note concluded with a revelation of its meaning:

"Before humanity, before history, and before its own conscience the Imperial Government does not wish to take the responsibility of renouncing any means, whatever they may be, of hastening the end of the war. It had hoped to be able to attain this end by negotiations with the President of the United States. Our adversaries having responded to this conciliatory step by the announcement of an aggravation of hostilities, it became necessary for the Imperial Government to continue the struggle, thus newly imposed upon it, by having recourse to all their arms, if they would serve the high ideal of humanity and hold themselves blameless towards their compatriots.

"Consequently, the Imperial Government decided to abolish the restrictions that it had hitherto imposed in the use of its means of naval warfare, in the hope that the American people and its Government would understand the causes and the necessity of this decision.

"The Imperial Government hopes that the United States will judge the new order of things from the high tribunal of impartiality, and that, on their side, they will also help to prevent further evils and the inevitable sacrifice of human life."

Three days later, on February 3rd, the President summoned the two Houses and the members of the Supreme Court to the Capitol. At two o'clock he appeared before them. He recalled the promise he had obtained from Germany a year earlier. He recalled the declaration he had made, that if Germany broke her engagement the United States would have no choice but to sever diplomatic relations with the Government of the German Empire altogether. Germany had broken her word. The President did not ask Congress to sever relationship with her. He had already done so. "I, therefore, directed the Secretary of State to announce to his Excellency the German Ambassador that all diplomatic relations between the United States and the German Empire are severed and that the American Ambassador in Berlin will immediately be withdrawn, and in accordance with this decision to hand to his Excellency his passports."

The Constitution authorised the President to decide upon a diplomatic rupture. Thus he was able, without exceeding his powers, to engage the nation in a war Congress alone had the right to decree. This war he had already predicted and shown from afar.

"If my inveterate confidence in the discretion and foresight of my intentions is unhappily proved to be without foundation; if American ships and American lives should in fact be sacrificed by German naval commanders in heedless contravention of the just and reasonable understandings of international law and the obvious dictates of humanity, I shall take the liberty of coming again before Congress to ask that authority be given to me to use any means that may be necessary for the protection of our seamen and our people in the prosecution of their peaceful legitimate errands on the high seas."

The descent into war was certain. President Wilson, as commander-in-chief of the forces on land and sea, armed merchant ships and gave each one military protection. He issued instructions that they were to fire on German submarines without allowing them time to attack. Germany declared that these armed guards would be treated as irregulars, and would be shot. From the month of March war existed in very fact, and there remained nothing more but to confirm it by formal vote.

At this moment the authority and prestige of the President were at their highest. The solemnities surrounding the renewal of his term of office were carried out amidst great national enthusiasm. In accordance with custom, on March 7th he appeared on the steps of the Capitol and addressed the gigantic crowd surging round the building.

"Here, in your midst, I stand and have taken the high solemn oath to which you have been audience because the people of the United States have chosen me for this august delegation of power, and by their gracious judgment have named me their leader in affairs. I know now what the task means. I realise to the full the responsibility which it involves. I pray God that I be given wisdom and prudence to do my duty in the true spirit of this great people. I am their servant, and can succeed only as they sustain and guide me by their confidence and their counsel.

"The thing I shall count upon and the thing without which neither counsel nor action avail is the unity of America—an America united in feeling, in purpose, in its vision of duty and its opportunity of service.

"We have to beware of all men who would turn the tasks and necessities of the nation to their own private profit or use them for the upbuilding of private power. Beware that no faction or disloyal intrigue break the harmony or embarrass the spirit of our people. Beware that our Government be kept pure and incorrupt in all its parts. United alike in the conception of our duty and in the high resolve to perform it in face of all men, let us dedicate ourselves to the great task to which we must now set our hand.

"For myself I beg your tolerance, your countenance, your united aid. The shadows that now lie dark upon our path will soon be dispelled. We shall walk with light all about us if we be but true to ourselves—to ourselves as we have wished to be known in the counsels of the world, in the thought of all those who love liberty, justice, and right exalted."

What he asked for now he was sure to obtain. All hearts were with him. On April 2nd he called Congress together in extraordinary session, and asked for a vote for war:

"Armed neutrality, it now appears, is impracticable. Because submarines are in effect outlaws when used as the German submarines have been used against merchant shipping, it is impossible to defend ships against their attacks as the law of nations has assumed that merchantmen would defend themselves against privateers or cruisers, visible craft giving chase upon the open sea. It is common prudence in such circumstances, grim necessity indeed, to endeavour to destroy them before they have shown their own intention. They must be dealt with upon sight, if dealt with at all. The German Government denies the right of neutrals to use arms at all within the areas of the sea which it has proscribed, even in the defence of rights which no modern publicist has ever before questioned their right to defend. The intimation is conveyed that the armed guards which we have placed on our merchant ships will be treated as beyond the pale of law and subject to be dealt with as pirates would be. Armed neutrality is ineffectual enough at best; in such circumstances and in the face of such pretensions it is worse than ineffectual; it is likely only to produce what it was intended to prevent; it is practically certain to draw us into the war without either the rights or the effectiveness of belligerents. There is one choice we cannot make, we are incapable of making: we will not choose the path of submission and suffer the most sacred rights of our nation and our people to be ignored or violated. The wrongs against which we now array ourselves are no common wrongs: they cut to the very roots of human life.

"With a profound sense of the solemn and even tragical character of the step I am taking and of the grave responsibilities which it involves, but in unhesitating obedience to what I deem my constitutional duty, I advise that the Congress declare the recent course of the Imperial German Government to be in fact nothing less than war against the government and people of the United States; that it formally accept the status of belligerent which has thus been thrust upon it; and that it take immediate steps not only to put the country in a more thorough state of defence but also to exert all its power and employ all its resources to bring the Government of the German Empire to terms and end the war."

In addition the President asked for an allocation of credit on behalf of the Powers already in conflict with Germany, the placing of the fleet on a war footing, the economic mobilisation of national resources and labour, and an immediate increase of the army. He asked for 500,000 recruits upon the principle of universal obligatory service. But what he did not ask for, what he did not say in actual words, he allowed to be understood. In the continuation of his speech he said, "We must help the Powers warring against Germany." (He always avoided calling them the Allied Powers —but perhaps the word is not important.) Then he added, and in reproducing the phrase the press underlined it, "These Powers are in the field. We must help them in every manner that can be effective."

The deed was done. We need not tell the story of the resistance, the parliamentary manœuvres always being resumed and always being disappointed. We need not attempt to analyse the war organisation which added to the already immense powers of the President, associating him with the technical councils which already held considerable authority. The facts are not yet at the disposition of the historian. A moment must be given to that afternoon of June 14th when the President celebrated "Flag Day" in the presence of the people. A policeman had to hold an umbrella over his head as he spoke, for it was raining. Yet his speech was so ardent that the crowd was deeply impressed. He wished them to know exactly where they were going, warned them that they were engaged in the most formidable of fights.

"My Fellow Citizens:
"We meet to celebrate Flag Day because this flag which we honour and under which we serve is the emblem of our unity, our power, our thought and purpose as a nation. It has

no other character than that which we give it from generation to generation. The choices are ours. It floats in majestic silence above the hosts that execute those choices, whether in peace or in war. And yet, though silent, it speaks to us—speaks to us of the past, of the men and women who went before us and of the records they wrote upon it. We celebrate the day of its birth; and from its birth until now it has witnessed a great history, has floated on high the symbol of great events, of a great plan of life worked out by a great people. We are about to carry it into battle, to lift it where it will draw the fire of our enemies. We are about to bid thousands, hundreds of thousands, it may be millions, of our men, the young, the strong, the capable men of the nation, to go forth and die beneath it on fields of blood far away—for what? For some unaccustomed thing? For something for which it has never sought the fire before? American armies were never before sent across the seas. Why are they sent now? For some purpose, for which this great flag has never been carried before, or for some old, familiar, heroic purpose for which it has seen men, its own men, die on every battlefield upon which Americans have borne arms since the Revolution? . . ."

Again the President defined the cause the United States were defending. He finished with a promise and a threat.

"For us there is but one choice. We have made it. Woe be to the man or group of men that seeks to stand in our way in this day of high resolution when every principle we hold dearest is to be vindicated and made secure for the salvation of the nations. We are ready to plead at the bar of history, and our flag shall wear a new lustre. Once more we shall make good with our lives and fortunes the great faith to which we were born, and a new glory shall shine in the face of our people."

Woe be to the man who seeks to stand in our way! Many liberals, until then eager in their support of the President, disliked this threat, and did not hide their censure. The President left them to their talk. He knew better than these enthusiastic but weak critics the task he had undertaken. Exercised by power and developed by responsibility his spirit penetrated a future still shrouded in shadow. He was able to imagine the unprecedented sacrifices he was about to exact, the opposition, the crises, the anarchist anger, he would be compelled to break. The conquering Lincoln fell under the

bullet of a fanatic, as the President well knew.
He was better qualified than any of the liberals to measure the formidable problem of allowing a young, fresh, and passionate nation
to enter the sanguinary arena. With full
knowledge he assumed the task. But, to carry
it through, he had to call for the exercise of
every one of his rights.

He obtained them. In September, Congress
adjourned, after having long resisted and pro-
longed its debates. President Wilson now
stood alone. He was head of the armies on
land and on sea, dictator of production and
consumption, absolute master over every battle and of all labour. His powers of action
were of the widest and the law itself sanctioned
his decrees. "It has taken four months to
clear the decks," wrote the *North American
Review* in September, 1917. "They are cleared
now. Despite the haggling and hobbling of a
Congress unwilling to invoke clôture to make
effective the will of a majority, despite the
hundred days of futile debate upon a single bill
imposed by a few wilful men under sinister
leadership of extraordinary skill, the true
theory of undivided, masterful direction in war
has finally prevailed, and the President holds
in the hollow of his hands the full power which

should have been his from the beginning,—a power infinitely greater than that of any other living ruler and unsurpassed by that of Alexander or of Napoleon."

In this manner the entire nation viewed the leader it had elected as its head. "Now he is free," ran the word in clubs, streets, newspapers, homes, "the war will be won."